The
Simplicity
of
Homeschooling

by
Vicky Goodchild

The Simplicity of Homeschooling
Discover the Freedom of Learning through Living
Published by HIS Publishing Company

© 1997 by Vicky Goodchild
Second printing 1999
Cover design by Gay Knight

Printed in the United States of America

International Standard Book Number (ISBN): 0-9626448-1-1

DEDICATION

To Tim, Kimberly, Stephen, Laura, and Michelle
You are what it's all about!

———————————◆———————————

If we work upon marble, it will perish; if on brass,
time will efface it; if we rear temples, they will
crumble into dust; but if we work upon immortal
minds, and imbue them with principles, with the
just fear of God and love of our fellow men, we
engrave on those tablets something that will
brighten to all eternity.

— Webster

In Appreciation...

It would be impossible to acknowledge everyone who has influenced my family's lives regarding homeschooling. Fourteen years of conversations and readings have all played a role in conforming our views into what they are today. Each has a special face behind it, so in a sense this book is more than just our story. To those who have shared and stimulated our ideas and beliefs we say a heartfelt, Thank You!

We would like to especially acknowledge Dr. Raymond and Dorothy Moore (the grandparents of the home school movement) and also Wade and Jessica Hulcy and Charles and Carole Thaxton of KONOS. Their friendships and writings have been especially influential. There are also the writings of such home school greats as Charlotte Mason, Susan Schaeffer Macaulay, and Ruth Beechick. Each one has tremendously shaped our thinking.

The writings of Susan Macaulay's father and mother, Frances and Edith Schaeffer, have influenced our thinking in the area of Christian worldview, family, and creativity. The writings, the songs, and the hours of "philosophizing" with our good friends Monte and Karey Swan have had a tremendous impact on us in the area of homemaking beyond maintenance and the homeschool lifestyle.

Then there are those very special people who are a part of our everyday lives — those we can always count on not only for advice, encouragement, and prayer, but also unconditional love, a good laugh, and deep friendship. These include our parents, Clarence and Etta Norman, and Dick and Ruth Goodchild. Your lives have modeled integrity, credibility, and consistency and we are stronger for it. We pray we will model the same for our children. Also my very dear friends Judy Linzie and Gay Knight (who also happens to be my sister). You are both such a blessing. You know me better than most and still stay true. And to our precious children — Tim, Kimberly, Stephen, Laura, and Michelle — as your father and I teach you, we learn so much about what is truly important. Thanks for your patience and cooperation. I'm back now!

I also thank Jack, my husband, for his encouragement, support, and patience during this project. When he asked me to write this, I think he didn't realize what we were in for. He believed in me and this book even when I felt like giving up. Thanks Honey!

My deepest thanks goes to the Lord. Thank you for setting our family on this path and for graciously guiding and teaching us day-by-day. We couldn't do it without You!

Special thanks to those who read the earlier draft of this book and lent us their valuable insights: Mom and Dad Norman, Gay Knight, Judy Linzie, Bob and Tina Farewell, Ruth Beechick, Dorthy Moore, Jessica Hulcy, Pam Lancaster, Karey Swan, Kathy von Duyke, and Dave and Joan Exley. You are all very dear to me.

I believe people are who they are by the influences in their lives. If you see anything worthwhile, thank the Lord first and then those who have unselfishly shared their lives with our family.

If instead of a gem, or even a flower, we should cast the gift
of a loving thought into the heart of a friend,
that would be giving as the angels give.
— George MacDonald

Tea and Sympathy...

To me tea has a warm, soothing, calming effect. It evokes a nostalgia of by-gone days. Mostly it symbolizes friendship... relationship! My dear Dutch friend, Jantena, taught me how to "take tea." Her affectionate word for it is "cuppa," and we know it means we will take a few special moments to share whatever is on our hearts and our friendship will be deeper and richer for the time we spent together. Now, sadly, we are 1,500 miles apart, but we still partake of our "cuppa" through the words we share in our letters. It doesn't feel quite right if I don't have a cup of tea in one hand while her letter is in the other.

I have sipped countless cups of tea (and coffee) during the writing of this book, and it seems only fitting to share one with you now. It has been my experience that having a cup of tea with a friend is an effective way to confirm ideas and calm doubts, fears, and confusion. So go make a cup of your favorite warm beverage, and let's have a "cuppa" as we chat through these pages and hope to meet face to face one day.

Vicky

A Teatime Blessing

Lord, you have assigned me my portion and my cup;
You have made my lot secure.
The boundary lines have fallen for me in pleasant places;
Surely I have a delightful inheritance.

— Psalms 16:5-6

To Husbands

Forgive me if it sounds like I'm speaking only to your wife. I hope you will read this book too, and I know many of you will. However during fourteen years of counseling homeschool families, I have all too many times heard wives sigh about the fact that they can't get their husbands to read the things which have been enlightening or inspiring to them. I understand the reasons why, yet if I might be so bold, I would tell you that your wife will need your support and encouragement for this family endeavor. I'm so grateful for Jack's sensitivity to my needs and the children's needs. He is the stabilizing force that gently moves us toward our family's goals, always mindful of the tender hearts and relationships for which he is responsible. May I suggest that you read this book with your wife, so you may benefit from the same frame of reference and from the delightful effects of a shared "cuppa."

My dear, if you could give me a cup of tea to clear my muddle
of a head, I should better understand your affairs.
— Charles Dickens

TABLE OF CONTENTS

INTRODUCTION

⸺◆⸺

The *simplicity of homeschooling?* Is there really such a thing? Certainly homeschooling is no *simple* task. Any honest homeschooler would admit to that. Then, where does simplicity fit in? First, I must clarify that I'm not speaking of becoming *simplistic*, which indicates oversimplification. This is actually a false simplicity which ignores the complicating factors (of which there can be many). *Simplicity*, however, *seeks to reduce* (not ignore) *the unnecessary complexities and provide clarity of purpose*.

Unfortunately, far too many homeschoolers view the combined use of the words simplicity and homeschooling as nothing short of a paradox. Their personal experiences and example to others have never suggested this as a possibility. Fortunately, a paradox is only a seeming inconsistency, not a true one.

If the title of this book seems inconsistent to you, I would guess you are either a new or prospective homeschooler who is confused with all the curriculum choices, legalities, and pressure from friends and extended family or a veteran homeschooler who feels burned out and on the verge of defeat. If you, or someone you know, fits into either of these categories, I would urge you to read on. This book is for you!

GOOD NEWS

The good news is that your home school can be a joyful, rewarding adventure! It can be all you ever hoped it could be. It can provide a nourishing environment for building godly character and positive social interaction and it can provide a superior education for your children. It can build relationships among family members that have meaning and endurance. And, all this can happen in an environment free from daily stress, tension, and complications — well, almost. To be sure, there will be challenges and both victories and defeats. If there were no challenges or defeats we wouldn't have a standard by which to

> Educating our children doesn't have to be a complicated process, it just needs to be a thoughtful process.
> —Valerie Bendt, *How to Create Your Own Unit Study*

measure the victories. However, many homeschoolers experience the same defeats over and over again. Moving toward simplicity will arrest this dangerous pattern which leads to discouragement and burn-out.

As veteran homeschoolers for 14 years, our family can attest to the fact that the attainment of simplicity was not without a painful struggle. Through a distillation process which included years of trial and error, successes and failures, tears and laughter, and hours and hours of prayer, we have concluded that at the heart of finding simplicity in our homeschooling experience is the development of our family's *learning lifestyle*.

In this book, you will be introduced to a style of educating that promises freedom, simplicity, and joy in learning. It is something we have come to call a *Learning Lifestyle*. Simply defined it is *learning through living*. Approaching learning as a lifestyle has allowed us to move beyond the parameters of what is typically thought of as education and has provided an atmosphere for learning that has exceeded any of our expectations. It has served to reduce the complexities rather than ignore them. Ignoring the complexities doomed us to their repetition and the sense of endless wallowing in the same dull rut. Conversely, learning through living gives fresh life and clarity of purpose to our learning each day. This is not to say we never have any doubts, worries, or problems. However, we can say, we have far fewer.

To The New Homeschooler

My goal in writing this book is to help you wade through as many mistakes as possible, on the pages of this book, rather than through personal experience. It doesn't mean your situation will always be a bed of roses; among those petals there are sure to be a few thorns. Experience is still one of the best teachers. However, if you are willing to learn from others' mistakes, it could result in plucking away a great number of those thorns before you get pricked.

Also, for the new homeschooler (and possibly veterans who are unaware), I have provided a verbal timeline of the modern homeschool movement, first from a personal perspective and then from the perspective of methods. This should help you understand the *language* you will hear spoken in homeschool

There is no gathering the rose without being pricked by the thorns.

— Pilpay

circles and at conventions. It will also equip you to make informed decisions regarding the purchase of resources necessary to reach your family's goals.

TO THE VETERAN HOMESCHOOLER

My aim for you (especially for those of you feeling weary or burned out), is to provide you with encouragement and a challenge to take a fresh look at *homeschooling as a lifestyle rather than simply a system of education.*

CONFIRMATION

During the writing of this book (actually very near its completion) it has been interesting to come across other authors who are expressing very similar conclusions about their homeschool experience. It is also interesting that, although we don't know each other, we are all using very similar terminology. I believe this is not a coincidence. Rather, I believe it confirms how God is answering the prayers of many and leading us all toward a richer homeschool experience which nurtures the family and will ultimately lead to a stronger society.

Although I have been able to peruse only some of these books or simply listen to summaries by friends, I intend to read them in their entirety after I complete this book. I recommend you do the same (see Chapter Three). I would be the first to admit that I don't have all the answers. To be honest, I struggled with the necessity of writing this and almost backed out, figuring it has already been said. However, I became convinced (in ways only God can achieve), that it is essential for the homeschool community to hear from several perspectives to reinforce the message, as well as demonstrate the fact that this style of learning adjusts to the uniqueness of each family.

Whether you are teaching toddlers, teens, anywhere in between, or all of the above, I hope this publication helps you find simplicity in homeschooling, provides direction in discovering your family's learning lifestyle, and results in you experiencing the freedom of learning through living.

> Homeschooling is a lifestyle — not simply a system of education.

HELPFUL TIPS FOR USING THIS BOOK

TIP #1: MARGINS

The margins on the outside of the text have been provided for your personal notes or additional information you may want to add to this manual. I hope you will find this book serves as your "file cabinet" for frequently-used information. It is intended to be used as a handy reference, not simply to be read and placed on a shelf. Since some of you have a hard time getting yourself to write in a book, I hereby give you permission to mark it up, make notes, underline, and highlight. Only *you* can truly make it functional!

TIP #2: RECOMMENDED RESOURCES

When I began homeschooling the problem was a lack of resources. Today the problem is the abundance of resources. Too many choices complicate the process. The resources I have listed are those I feel confident recommending because they have worked well for us or for those whose opinions I highly regard. I hope I don't offend anyone because I haven't listed their favorites. I know there are other quality materials available, however, I have chosen to keep my lists short to discourage confusion. Compare my choices to the endorsements from your friends or helpful homeschool catalogs. In the end, you must make intelligent choices to meet the needs of *your* family. However, the best advice is to allow God to be your ultimate guide.

TIP #3: OBTAINING RESOURCES

Throughout this book you will come across recommended resources. Nothing is more frustrating to me than to read about a great resource and then have no idea how to go about obtaining it. Appendix B deals with that issue. You will find there a list of suppliers compiled in alphabetical order. I highly recommend that you call or write for all the catalogs which I have designated as general homeschool mail-order catalogs. Each carries a wide variety of materials that reflect the philosophy or experiences of the owners' own homeschools. Of particular interest are the teaching tips which each one provides. You will obtain a wealth of knowledge by simply reading the catalogs. Be careful however, to sift the information in light of *your* family's goals and needs. Resist the temptation to purchase unnecessary materials. *If you are interested in simplicity, you must streamline your resources.*

TIP #4: COST OF RESOURCES

I have tried to provide a price for each resource. Please be aware that all the prices are subject to change at any time. I listed these just to give you a general idea of costs involved since, for example, phonics programs range anywhere from $4 to $200. Curriculum suppliers are in no way obligated to meet these quoted prices.

TIP #5: TERMINOLOGY

You will notice that the terms homeschool, homeschooling, and homeschoolers will be used interchangeably with home educate, home educating, and home educators. Also, to avoid having to constantly write he/she, him/her, and his/her, the pronouns he, him, and his are used throughout.

CHAPTER ONE

——•••◆•••——

ME?! HOMESCHOOL?!

How well I remember the Spring of 1983… My mind wandered back through the three short years that had passed since I completed what would be my last year of teaching in a public high school. Our first pregnancy during the '79-'80 school year found Jack and me making the decision that it would be best for me to stay home to raise our newborn — at least until our child was school age. We would reevaluate as that time came closer. Jack's mom had always been at home when he arrived from school each day and so had mine. We were sure this would be important for the well-being of our child too. Besides, I was finally realizing my heart's desire — a child of my own and full-time mothering.

I had never been one to desire a career. I remember thinking that a teaching degree might be a good thing to fall back on if the need ever arose, however my real desire was to raise a family. One day as I watched my energetic 2½-year-old moving from one activity to the next, pondering, figuring, exploring, and trying to express his thoughts, my own mind reeled with both confusion and excitement because of the book I held in my hand. My sister had loaned me a book on education that she had found in the library, and she insisted I read it. I figured she wanted a "professional's" opinion. Little did I know how reading the book, *Home Grown Kids*, by Dr. Raymond and Dorothy Moore, would forever change the course of our lives (or rather the course I thought our lives would take).

I had envisioned myself being a loyal card-carrying member of the PTA. I'd bake cupcakes as any faithful homeroom mother would. I would be the first to volunteer for chaperoning

Home —
where life makes
up its mind.
—Chuck Swindoll

field trips. I would be available to help with homework. I was going to be *involved* in my child's education! But — this involved? Gulp!

Who ever heard of teaching your own child at home? Was it even legal? I wasn't certified in elementary education. I had only taken one elementary education course in college because it was required. I never wanted to teach a child to read and write and do basic math. "No. No! This is impossible, unheard of, don't even entertain the thought," I told myself. Yet the studies that Dr. and Mrs. Moore cited regarding readiness, negative socialization, and mass-produced education haunted me. I had witnessed the sad effects of these on the high school kids I had taught in the public school system.

I tentatively began sharing my new findings with Jack, not sure whether he would agree with the Moores (meaning a 180-degree turn for me) or give the final axe to the matter (meaning I could dismiss the whole idea in good conscience). He agreed whole-heartedly with the Moores! But, surely our parents would disapprove! After sharing the findings and sharing our hearts, both sets of parents/grandparents became, and continue to be, our most loyal supporters. Gulp again! So began our homeschool adventure.

Despite all I had read supporting delayed academics, I thought we would help our bright, three-year-old son, Timmy, get a jump-start on his education. Or, maybe it was just the four years of indoctrination I received in college that made me order that pre-school curriculum. By the time it arrived we were ready to leave on a one-month vacation up the east coast of the U.S. What good timing, I thought! I could begin teaching school on our trip. Mind you, Timmy was still riding in a car seat. After just a short time into the trip I pulled out the box to make my initial inspection and begin writing my lesson plans. My heart sank! This looked boring, even to me. At that moment I made one of the best decisions I've ever made and it came purely from a mother's instinct. I packed up the box, slid it under a seat, and left it there until we returned home and I could ship it back to the company, post haste!

So, did Timmy experience any learning that month? You better believe it! He explored, imagined, pretended, investi-

Imagination is more important than knowledge.
— Albert Einstein

gated, identified, questioned, dialogued, discovered, and had loads of fun during this normally inquisitive year of his life. He was also forming something that Mrs. Moore described as *learning hooks*. He was storing plenty of information that would later be useful to hang new ideas and pieces of information upon. And to think I had considered stifling those endeavors in exchange for filling out endless worksheets!

Little did I realize that I was also developing learning hooks. I was beginning to see that learning would take place in spite of me and all my well-intentioned plans. I had just learned a major lesson. During the next fourteen years I would return to this *hook* (and its successive links) many times to verify the fact that our children's Creator had indeed created them with sufficient wonder and awe to enable them to learn and grow into the individuals He created them to be.

Shortly after we returned from that trip, Jack and I met some other like-minded parents and learned of a way we could legally home educate. It would require establishing a private school. It was a gray area of the law but it was working for others in our state and we thought we would try it too. Since our son was not yet compulsory attendance age we didn't need to worry too much. However, we feared facing truancy charges if we didn't make sure something legal was in place before he turned six. Jack and I and three other couples established a private school for home-schoolers. The families registered their children in the private school, yet still used their homes as their campus. Thus began our stint as private school administrators. We also began a support group that grew from ten families to 100 families in just a year. We were often asked to do radio and television interviews on both secular and religious stations. In our county, our name was becoming synonymous with this radical and crazy thing called homeschooling.

I remember how ecstatic I was when I heard that the Moores would be in Florida to hold seminars. Not only did we attend the one in our area but, just like regular groupies, we drove four hours north the following weekend to attend the workshops in Orlando. Once again I was challenged to adjust my educational philosophy from what I had learned in my college classroom to what I knew to be true from observing our own child.

Knowledge is a pure delight... Let his lessons approach him on the lines of his nature — not on the lines proper for certain subjects of instruction — and the little boy has no choice. He cannot help learning and loving to learn, " 'cos 'tis his nature to."
— Charlotte Mason

That Orlando meeting was when our state organization, The Florida Parent Educators Association (FPEA), was established. We confirmed our support through the elbow grease we applied. Our names were now known on a state level. Keep in mind, this was not a pleasant proposition since at that time most families were doing everything they could to remain anonymous.

About a year later, I remember a small group of us being called in to speak with Dr. D. James Kennedy of Coral Ridge Presbyterian Church and Dr. Ken Wackes of Westminster Academy (the private school associated with Coral Ridge) to discuss impending legislation that would virtually stop homeschooling in its tracks. Our state's Education Commissioner had proposed legislation that would allow parents to homeschool, only if we would consent to annual psychological evaluations. Dr. Wackes and Dr. Kennedy warned us of the dangerous ramifications and offered support in whatever way they could. Their encouragement and prayers helped to carry us through a tumultuous year of legislative battles.

During the 1985 legislative session, the struggle to secure a good home education law began. It was exciting to be a part of the lobbying efforts in Tallahassee and witness the legislative process in action. Working shoulder to shoulder with the likes of Craig and Brenda Dickinson (the late Craig Dickinson authored the bill in opposition to the Commissioner's bill) and Representative Dan Webster, (bill sponsor, homeschool father, and current Speaker of the House) was both exciting and frightening. We were soon to find out how desperately the National Education Association (NEA) wanted to defeat this bill. We also witnessed how the merciful hand of a loving God directed the bill through each phase of the process. While the NEA laughed at us, the bill passed both houses of the legislature. Sadly, it was placed on a list of recommended vetoes. The governor consented to a *brief* visit with a few homeschoolers and after about an *hour* he agreed to sign the bill. It was truly a miracle that he would not only go against a bill proposed by someone on his cabinet, but that such a controversial piece of legislation could be passed in only one session.

Back home again we encouraged the folks in our county to comply with our new law. We closed the private school, yet continued the support group. Through the commitment and hard work of a number of wonderful leaders it has continued to grow and currently has a membership of over 500 families. Likewise, the support networks in each state have been vital to establishing and maintaining positive legislation throughout America.

Now that our freedoms were relatively secure, it was time for our family to focus on our personal strategy for homeschooling. Contrary to the way in which many families were teaching at the time, my instincts led me to choose a topic of interest and study it until we were satisfied. At a 1986 curriculum fair I was introduced to *KONOS Curriculum* and learned that what I was doing was teaching via "unit studies." The authors, Jessica Hulcy and Carole Thaxton, had gone to great lengths to study this method, compare it to how children learn best, and then prepared several units. I was so excited to find some help with how I was already teaching, I not only bought the curriculum for our family, but began to sell it to others. We would be on the curriculum fair circuit for years to come.

By 1990, it seemed as if every homeschooler and potential homeschooler in Florida had our phone number. While I dearly loved ministering to the homeschool community, I felt I was neglecting my own family. At that point we had three children and I was in the "serious" stages of home educating our oldest child and also adding new children to the family. Realizing that I was answering the same questions over and over again, the idea of writing a book was suggested by our pastor who was sensing my frustration. The book was called *An Orientation to Home Schooling in Florida*. The book you are now reading is a revision and very expanded version of that book. It excludes the information that is only pertinent to Florida and includes information based on an additional seven years of experience. You will find these experiences scattered throughout the contents of this book.

As we continued on the Florida curriculum fair circuit, I continued to speak on various topics and we began to add the books to our display that had been helpful to us and which we felt would encourage other homeschoolers. Shortly thereafter, Jack started our mail-order catalog business called HIS Publishing Company. We operated the retail end of our small cottage industry for about a total of ten years. During that time we had the privilege of counseling thousands of homeschool families. Soon our "small" cottage industry grew larger than we felt was practical for our family (Jack is also a full-time, professional firefighter for our city). In our effort to simplify our lives (and maintain our sanity), we chose to close down the mail-order division of our company and concentrate on the small-scale publishing of our own materials.

Presently (1997) our family has five children ranging from teen to toddler. Me? Homeschool?! Yes, even I, with all of my predetermined educational baggage, somehow saw the sense in it fourteen years ago, and now even more emphatically see the necessity of it. I know there are some who will say, "Sure! She can do it — she's a teacher. I'm just a mom with no special training. My child deserves a professional!" That is probably the biggest deception that has been fed to the parents of America. You may not be *certified* but you are definitely *qualified!* That' s why God created parents.

Before typical school entry, most parents have taught their child a language, many social graces, letters, colors, numbers, and countless other skills. There is no magic childhood age when a "professional" is required. *You* are your child's qualified professional. No one cares more for your child than you. If you are a warm, responsive, loving parent, YOU CAN homeschool. Of course it helps if you are able to read and write and do basic math but even those are not insurmountable obstacles. If you expect your children to learn, then you can certainly train yourself or find a tutor to train you. One mother in our area is blind and yet successfully homeschools her children. Deep concern for our child's best has driven many of us to overcome handicaps or to learn skills and topics we never felt we would be capable of tackling. And on some occasions, when we truly feel incapable (I have Chemistry-phobia), we barter our talents or hire tutors to help us.

I know countless parents from diverse backgrounds who are successfully homeschooling their children. The common denominator for success is not based on the amount of family income (both rich and poor can successfully homeschool) or the degree of education the parents have (both college graduates and high school drop-outs successfully homeschool). In my analysis, the common denominator is the amount of *desire* and degree of *determination* a family has to make this work for them. Take for example a friend of mine who dropped out of high school during the tenth grade. Many years later, when her first child successfully graduated from their homeschool program, she decided to get her GED. She scored higher than anyone in the history of that particular testing facility. She even received money toward a college scholarship because of her high marks. She says she learned far more from home educating her own children than from the school system she attended as a child.

One of the most unique yet unifying features of the homeschool movement is the diversity among its participants. We all come from such different backgrounds. We bring with us our personal experiences, values, and belief systems that create the very fiber from which each homeschool tapestry will be woven. Each will be unique yet each has the ability to produce the success stories that I believe has the potential to change America. Read more about the success stories of diverse homeschooling families in *Homespun Schools* (1982) $8.00 and *The Successful Home School Family Handbook* (1994) $13.00, both by Dr. Raymond and Dorothy Moore and available from general homeschool mail-order catalog companies (see Appendix B).

By the way, if you are ever tempted to obtain a teaching degree because you think it will help you to better educate your children, I would caution you to rethink the matter. Most home educators I know who have teaching degrees (myself included), agree that many times it is a liability rather than an asset. Much of our training was related to the "herd mentality" (everyone learns the same thing, the same way, at the same time) and how to discipline the masses. Homeschooling is so very different! My biggest hurdle was *unlearning* information which had greatly handicapped me. I still struggle in some areas. On the other hand, there are many reasons why I am grateful for my education background. However, my point here is that it isn't necessary for successful homeschooling. As a matter of fact, Dr. Brian Ray of the National Home Education Research Institute (NHERI) released the results (March, 1997) of the largest study of homeschooling ever conducted. The study is being published in book form and is titled *Strengths of Their Own - Home Schoolers Across America: Academic Achievement, Family Characteristics, and Longitudinal Traits*, by Dr. Brian Ray, $19.95. This study was commissioned by the Home School Legal Defense Association. Among other findings, Michael Farris (President of HSLDA) and Dr. Ray announced at a press conference (March 5, 1997) that the study revealed teacher certification of parents does not significantly influence homeschooled students' performance. Even when homeschooling moms are not high school graduates, their children still score higher on standardized tests than the average public school student. This should finally put everyone's mind at ease concerning this issue. If you would like to order a copy of the entire study, contact NHERI (see Appendix B for contact information).

Closely related to this issue of teacher certification as a handicap, is the one most parents bring with them into the home school — a conventional classroom notion of education. This struggle is practically universal and all those affected must rethink the definition of true education — teaching children how to learn. Placing the effort on teaching children *how to learn* rather than merely presenting them with endless rote facts is a great stride toward finding *the simplicity of homeschooling.*

The essential qualifications of a great homeschool parent are built in. God handed you your certification papers the day you became a parent. He equipped you with the ability to train up your children in all aspects. Just as the Bible relates the experiences of others for our example, we can learn from the examples of veteran homeschoolers who have gleaned knowledge and insight from their years of experience with both victories and defeats. Take seriously your responsibility to read and investigate, and then learn how to plan and implement your homeschool. While nothing can take the place of self-education, do take advantage of your local and state support organizations' available training sessions during meetings, workshops, and conventions. Consider these your professional education classes. As with anything, read books (including this one) and attend lectures with a discerning heart and mind regarding what is best for your family.

I believe anyone who has a desire to, can homeschool! It is one of the most enjoyable, satisfying, and rewarding adventures we have experienced as a family. When approached as an extension of our responsibility to "train up our children," it becomes a

What is a family? A formation center for human relationships — worth fighting for, worth calling a career, worth the dignity of hard work.
— Edith Schaeffer
What Is a Family?

natural part of our lives. Has it always been easy? Definitely not! The training of our children (including homeschooling) ranks as the most challenging endeavor we have ever experienced. Homeschooling, like child training in general, will have its frustrating phases. Jack and I have begun to see those phases as our growing pains — times when we are about to experience growth spurts. These growth spurts always indicate changes that need to be made — changes in methods, schedules, discipline, or attitudes (mine and/or the children's). It was just such a time which led us to the realization of the simplicity of homeschooling as a learning lifestyle. Homeschooling has the unique ability to stretch us to what we think are our very limits and then somehow turn around and assure us we are doing exactly what we should be doing for our family, and that we wouldn't want it any other way.

Though it hasn't always been easy, it has always been worth it! We see it daily in the lives of our children. As they mature we are reaping the wonderful benefits we only dared to hope for — children who are intelligent, self-disciplined, obedient, kind, and responsible (at least most of the time). It has been a process that has taken time and patience. To some it may seem that the amount of time a homeschooling family spends together could provoke its undoing. On the contrary, it forces us to deal with issues and come to terms with them. It has taught us to love, forgive, and respect each other. It nurtures relationships that are forever sealed with love and commitment. As our good friend, Monte Swan often reminds us, "the only things eternal are our relationships."

For this reason we continue to feel called and even compelled to encourage others to take possibly the most challenging but definitely the most rewarding adventure ever taken — an adventure that changes families forever. As much as you might think it impossible, with love, commitment, and motivation even YOU CAN homeschool.

If we receive it, that the whole of education consists in the establishment of relations, then, the relations with our fellow-beings must be of the first importance.
— Charlotte Mason

CHAPTER TWO

---◆---

THE HISTORY OF HOMESCHOOL METHODS

When we began home schooling in 1983, there were three prevailing philosophies regarding methodology. As families began to incorporate (and literally experiment with) these methods, new methods began to be developed from a desire to meet individual family goals and to better complement particular home atmospheres. Some methods are spin-offs or combinations of the originals, while others are actually resurrected from the "old ways."

At this time, there are generally seven recognized methods. As you read the following descriptions, you will most likely experience a strong identification with one or more of the methods. My advice would be for you to resist your desire to embrace any one method until after you have considered Chapter Three. Afterwards, you may wish to investigate any of the methods in more detail by reading the accompanying resources that are recommended.

Please be aware that the presentation of these methods does not indicate mandates to be followed. Rather, they are considered here to help you understand how our present-day home school environment has evolved. Do not feel you must select one method over another, or even any of the methods. The very essence of home schooling is creativity and originality. Many home schoolers (our family included) tend to blend the best of all or most of the methods with a possible bent toward one or two particular brands. The "best" is what you interpret to be the best for your family, not the most convenient. Beware, however — some home educators are so adamant about "their way" that new home schoolers and veterans alike feel intimidated into following suit, even if it doesn't match their family lifestyle,

No two homeschools will be exactly alike. If you are determined to meet the needs of your child, you will do very well.

— Dr. Raymond and Dorothy Moore

educational philosophy, or individual goals. I can't stress enough that you must find the method or mesh of methods that works best for your family.

Don't be surprised if you find yourself abandoning one method after only six months to a year. It may be frustrating and you may feel this must indicate you are somehow a failure but let me reassure you by saying, probably 99% of all home schoolers do just that. Your family is in a constant state of change (ages, hobbies, likes/dislikes, career bents, skills) and you will need to be flexible and sometimes change methods to meet their changing needs.

During all my years as a homeschool educational consultant, I have witnessed the ebb and flow of each trend along with the evidence of its popularity underscored by the books that are published on the topic. Indeed, the copyright dates alone reveal the history. No doubt, other philosophies will emerge as the movement continues to grow. However, as you begin to accept homeschooling as a lifestyle rather than just another approach to education, you will be shielded from the dangerous rip currents that are produced as the various winds of "doctrine" begin to blow.

PREVAILING METHODS OF HOME EDUCATION

The first three methods in the following list were the prevailing methods of homeschooling which many found in place in the early 80's. The others are listed in the approximate order in which they have emerged in popularity and general acceptance among home schoolers. These are only brief descriptions but you can research them further by reading the recommended resources following each description.

THE CONVENTIONAL TEXTBOOK METHOD

This is the method we are all familiar with because most of us grew up on it. This conventional method uses textbooks or worktexts to teach each subject independent of each other and within a time frame each day (perhaps 50 minutes) until 180 days are completed for each school year. Teacher's manuals, tests, and answer keys are available.

Worktexts may be a new word to you. These are a series of workbooks that incorporate the text material. Included are related questions with blanks for answers, and all the required tests. There are several worktexts for each subject in each grade. The student moves to the next worktext after testing for mastery. The exclusive use of textbooks and worktexts practically necessitates that you run your homeschool similar to a conventional school.

Some families prefer to pick and choose from the available texts rather than purchasing a full grade level. This allows them to choose books based on their child's readiness and interests and to begin customizing their programs. Some parents choose textbooks for only one or two subjects to compliment their unit study program for the remaining subjects.

I would be remiss if I did not mention here that this method is extremely confining and restricts flexibility and creativity. It is primarily concerned with teaching and memorizing the facts that will presented on an achievement test. The exclusive use of textbooks, video classes, or computer schools generally tends to squelch a child's natural curiosity and love for learning and actually works counterproductive to your child's learning processes.

Many homeschoolers express a desire to start with this method based on their securities of the known versus the unknown. I must still caution you against the exclusive use of textbooks. I am not unsympathetic to your fears. I was in your shoes at one time. However, I am more concerned that you make the right start and avoid the many false starts and defeats that so many have experienced.

I am not against textbooks, as you may suppose. We use them when they are necessary to meet particular goals. It is the overuse and abuse of textbooks which I deplore. If used properly, textbooks, workbooks, computer courses, and video and audio cassette instruction can be used to build, test, and reinforce the basic skills and create a proficiency in them. Remember to let the workbooks and textbooks work for you and not against you, and never let them become a "busy-work" trap. Studies and experience show that you'll be setting yourself and your children up for burn-out (see *The Successful Homeschool Family*

If you find yourself struggling to mold your child to a book, try reversing priorities. It's the child you are teaching, not the book. Bend the book, or find another.
— Ruth Beechick, *You Can Teach Your Child Successfully*

17

Handbook, by Dr. Raymond and Dorothy Moore, $13.00). Here are some suggestions to help you make the best use of textbooks and workbooks:

1. Choose workbooks and textbooks that are at your child's ability level. Ability level is not always equivalent to grade level.

2. You do not have to work every problem on every page, unless you are signed up with a correspondence school and they require this. If a child has a clear understanding of the material, then it is not necessary to belabor the issue by doing countless pages of *practice* work.

3. It is not necessary to work in every workbook or subject every day. Change your routine and add some variety to your schedule.

4. Consider these your resources (something to fall back on for support) but never the focus of your homeschool.

    You can locate a list of suppliers in Appendix B.

The Delayed Academics Method

While the famous Head Start program (an early educational intervention program for preschoolers) was all the rage, Dr. Raymond and Mrs. Dorothy Moore were stating quite the opposite in their books *Better Late Than Early* (1975) and *School Can Wait* (1979). Going against the educational tide, their research concluded that children needed to have *formal education* (the systematic teaching of the 3 R's — reading, writing, and arithmetic) delayed rather than pursued earlier. The studies revealed that waiting on formal schooling would allow the child's "Integrated Maturity Level" (IML) to develop. A child's IML is developed when their brain, vision, hearing, perceptions, emotions, sociability, and physical growth come together to function cooperatively. All of these functions tend to mature at different levels but it is believed that for most children the point where the maturity levels integrate is no earlier than between the ages of 8 - 10 and then continue to mature through about the ages of 12 - 14. It was found that boys tend to mature later than girls in this area.

Dr. and Mrs. Moore are regarded by many as the pioneers of the modern homeschool movement. Their books *Home Grown Kids* (1981) and *Home Style Teaching* (1984) are the first books I read related to home education. That was when I became convinced that "readiness" was the key to wise education. I keenly recall this as an area of great concern during those early years. We were privileged to have Dr. and Mrs. Moore in our home when our oldest was just seven. I remember taking a walk with Mrs. Moore and grilling her on how to recognize "readiness." I wanted her to reveal the mystery formula. There is no such animal! There are, however, some recognizable signs. Curiosity about letters, books, and numbers indicates the first sign but by no means indicates the need for a full-scale curriculum. This is the point at which you gently answer your children's questions, read-aloud often, and provide real-life mathematical situations such as setting the table and counting butterflies in the backyard. I believe God, in His infinite wisdom, conceals the mystery formula from us so we will be ever-so-sensitive to our children's needs.

Mrs. Moore also indicated we shouldn't delay academics just for the sake of delay. If a child is begging to read and it doesn't frustrate him to learn the mechanics, by all means, teach the child to read. If he is ready earlier than others, that's O.K. too.

In addition to creating an awareness of readiness, the Moore's gave us the encouragement we needed to commit wholeheartedly to such a "radical" idea as homeschooling. And, they gave us the ammunition we needed (via their research) to thwart the "socialization" argument. The Moores were among the first to explain and advocate interest-based projects (a.k.a. unit studies) as the method of choice in home education. They not only provided the research data, but also the practical how-to's.

RECOMMENDED RESOURCES

Home Grown Kids, by Dr. Raymond and Dorothy Moore
General availability
Cost: $9.00

continued on following page

Provides the research, encouragement, and guidance to help you begin your homeschool.

Home Style Teaching, by Dr. and Mrs. Raymond Moore
Available through The Moore Foundation or
Lifetime Books and Gifts
Cost: $10.00
 This is the classic how-to homeschool manual. The methods are tried and true.

The Successful Homeschool Family Handbook, by Dr. Raymond and
  Dorothy Moore
General availability
Cost: $13.00
 Shows you how to implement a "Creative and Stress Free Approach to Homeschooling" (the subtitle). Novices and veterans alike will benefit. If you can only purchase one of their books I would recommend this one. It is a wonderful compilation of all their previous books.

The Moore Report International
Box 1, Camas, WA 98607 / (360) 835-2736
Cost: $12.00 / annual subscription. Arrives bi-monthly.
 A brief magazine which includes articles by the Moores, experiences of other homeschool families, and items of concern to the homeschool community.

THE UNSCHOOLING METHOD

John Holt was considered nothing less than an extreme radical when he wrote his book, *Teach Your Own* (1981 - published the same year as *Home Grown Kids*, by the Moores). After many years of work as an American educator he decided that the very methods being used to teach children were in actuality destroying their wonder and natural love for learning. His ideal of a method discarded any and all trappings of the conventional methods. He proposed that, given the opportunity, children will naturally learn what they need to know because of their desire to learn. This non-structured method is coupled with a learning environment which includes easy access to books and easy access to a caring adult who can answer the numerous questions sure to arise. Formal learning (including reading, writing, and arithmetic) is believed to happen when the child finds he needs it to further pursue his interests. The motivation and drive is "built in" and the child is poised for success.

While this method has wide appeal it has been primarily associated with non-Christian homeschoolers. It seems the dilemma for Christians is the fear of the home becoming too child-centered, resulting in a misplaced authority figure. The problem is that the Christians have thrown out the proverbial baby with the proverbial bath water and have swung way too far toward the other side of the pendulum. There is much to be gleaned from this method. Our family enjoys a style of learning which relies heavily on this method yet maintains the Biblical order of authority, discipline, structure, and boundaries. You will read about it in Chapter Three.

RECOMMENDED RESOURCES

Teach Your Own, by John Holt (1981)
John Holt's Book and Music Store Catalog or your local library.
  Cost: $16.95 (1997 edition)

Learning All the Time, by John Holt (1989)
General availability
Cost: $11.00

> Defines John Holt's beliefs about children and how they learn and includes how parents can encourage them in this process.

Homeschooling For Excellence, by David and Micki Colfax
General availability
Cost: $10.99

> A very encouraging "real-life" story of a homesteading family who allowed their four sons the freedom to follow their special interests and talents. The result: Harvard and Yale educations. This family was homeschooling in the 70's before the popular movement began.

Growing Without Schooling Magazine
2269 Massachusetts Ave., Cambridge, MA 02140 (617) 864-3100
Cost: $25.00 annual subscription. Arrives bi-monthly.

> Magazine founded by John Holt and has been carried on since his death, by supporters of the unschooling method. This is written from a secular perspective.

THE UNIT STUDY METHOD

Although it was not a new idea, but rather because it is the more natural way we all learn, the Moore's recommended this method in the early 80's as the most logical way to teach our children. A fair question might be, "If it is logical and natural then why don't parents naturally teach that way?" The most likely answer is that too many parents know of no other way to teach than the way in which they were taught. Nevertheless, many families experimented using this method and shared their good results with others. This eventually resulted in the availability of the many prepared unit study curricula on the market which evidences its popularity. Jack and I are particularly grateful for the pioneer work of Jessica Hulcy and Carole Thaxton in the area of prepared unit studies (authors of *KONOS Curriculum*). Because of their research and influence, our family has enjoyed

Give them more projects than workbooks... assignments that excite them and stretch their minds.
— Dr. Raymond and Dorothy Moore
Home Style Teaching

the many benefits associated with this style of learning. Our learning lifestyle relies heavily on this concept of learning in units.

So just what is the Unit Study Method? A unit study is simply an extensive study of one topic (or unit) and the integration of all subjects (social studies, science, language arts, math, Bible, music, art, etc.) around that topic. This allows the child to see the purpose for learning because the disciplines (subjects) are applied and the knowledge is interconnected, creating a more logical and natural way to learn. It is the opposite of the fragmented method of spending 50 minutes on history, which is totally unrelated to the next 50 minutes of science, which is totally unrelated to the next 50 minutes of literature, and so on.

It is important to point out that there are two ways to approach unit studies. We use both methods in our home. One method is to follow a parent-directed unit study which is prepared either by the parent or a unit study company. The second method is to allow the children to initiate their own units based on their interests or educational needs. They could be differentiated by defining the one as parent-directed, prepared unit studies and the other as student-directed, interest-based unit studies. While there are many similarities in the benefits and "whys" (the underlying principles), there are major differences in the "hows" (the presentation). The description under this method will deal with the parent-directed approach to prepared unit studies. For the description on student-directed, interest-based unit studies, see Chapter Three: The Learning Lifestyle.

Because this method is so highly favored and yet somewhat mysterious compared to what you were raised with, I have chosen to deal with this method extensively. Here is an example of a parent-directed unit study. Let's say your child loves baseball. You can create your curriculum around this and teach every subject. Just begin to brainstorm. The brainstorming can be done with your children which will result in them being able to accomplish this for themselves if you want them to be able to move into student-directed unit studies later on. Take one subject at a time and think about how baseball could relate to it. This is similar to what a prepared unit study curriculum will provide for you. The difference is that someone else has done the brainstorming and found the related resources for you.

SUBJECT:	ACTIVITIES AND QUESTIONS:
History	— Who invented baseball and how did it become such an American fascination? — Have the child read biographies about two of his favorite baseball players.
English	— Write a paper comparing and contrasting these two players. — Use this paper to learn editing, grammar, style, etc. — Compose a fictional short story about yourself being the world's greatest baseball player.
Literature	— Read *Casey at the Bat*, then dramatize the story.
Math	— Use baseball cards with stats to figure R.B.I.'s. — Compare players. — Subtract to find the difference between two players. — Add, then divide to find averages.
Geography	— Use a U.S. map to find all the home towns of the major league teams.
Government	— Are there any federal or local regulations pertaining to baseball players? — What about drug testing?
Health & Safety	— How do drugs affect a baseball player's physical skill, mental abilities, spiritual relationship to God, personal relationships with family members, etc. — Is baseball a safe game? How many injuries per year are reported?

Phys. Ed.	— Play baseball as a family. Honor the younger children by giving them the advantage. — Join a baseball team.
Science	— Learn about how a baseball is made. What types of materials and/or chemicals are used in its manufacturing. — Learn about the physics involved in throwing a curve ball, a fast ball, etc. — Study kinesthetic energy and velocity vs. resistance. (These I just heard about on an ABC World News Tonight report about baseball. This illustrates how you can incorporate every day information into your unit studies.)
Music	— Sing and learn the lyrics to "Take Me Out to the Ball Game." Who wrote it and how did it become so popular? — How did organ music become associated with baseball? — Compose your own song.
Art	— Sketch the illustrations for your fictional short story. — Were any baseball players known for their artistic abilities?
Character Development	— Many sports figures are looked up to as "heroes." Which baseball players do you think are "honorable" enough to be considered true heroes? — What are their life styles like? — Do they have faith in God? Do they live their faith under pressure? — Which players should not be emulated?

Spiritual
Development
— What Bible characters were honorable?
ex: Jesus, David, Moses, the Good Samaritan.
— As a family, read and dramatize the stories about these Bible characters.
— Play charades and guess who these Bible characters are.

Practical Living
and Fun
— Go to a baseball game as a family.
— Buy peanuts and crackerjacks and sing "Take Me Out to the Ball Game."

Prepared unit studies, whether devised by you or by a company, work especially well for small children through the elementary and junior high ages. (Student-directed unit studies are important during this stage too. See "The Learning Lifestyle" in Chapter Three). Working with a prepared curriculum gives experience and direction to the child regarding how to integrate their learning and pull together a body of knowledge from many sources. This is especially important for new homeschoolers who are accustomed to the textbook learning. We've used a prepared unit study curriculum since 1987 and have found the advantage to be that our high schooler can now create his own self-directed, interest-based units. This should be the goal of any teaching method... *to teach a child how to learn.*

A major goal in the Unit Study Method is to move away from the typical fragmentation of the disciplines (subjects). The object is to flow in and out of the subjects spontaneously rather than dealing with one at a time. Why? When the information is related to each other it gives meaning and purpose to the learning and results in an increased retention of knowledge. The information seems to be categorized and stored differently in the brain. This is in contrast to what happens when information is simply memorized for the sake of passing a test. I remember cramming for tests, spitting out the information, and then immediately forgetting. I remember that process but I don't remember much of the information I lost because of the process.

All the branches of knowledge are connected together, because the subject matter of knowledge is intimately united in itself, as being the acts and the work of the Creator.

— John H. Newman

You'll notice that the baseball example above lists the activities according to individual subjects. This is only to help you see how a general study of a topic can and will cover all of the disciplines. However, I do not propose that you follow the activities one after another. In reading the activities you will see how one activity extends over several disciplines. That is the essence of unit studies. When preparing a unit study you will want to encompass as many of the disciplines as possible, but don't be concerned if you can't think of activities for each one. Some topics don't lend themselves well to integrating every subject. For instance, a study on the electoral process at election time probably wouldn't include music and dance.

Spend as much time on a unit as you feel is appropriate, working a little each day or one full day a week. Most parents use the library where all the "textbooks" are free and there is a constant turn over in books rather than dealing with the foreboding feeling of having to complete that inch-thick text by the end of the year. An additional advantage to library usage is that the child learns not only how to use a library but also how to research. Don't be afraid to go off at a tangent when you find a particular aspect of your unit sparks curiosity and motivation. That, too, is part of the natural process of learning.

Most parent-directed or prepared unit studies recommend teaching the units multi-level. This simply means teaching all of the children the same unit at the same time yet at their own levels. The obvious advantage is that planning time is reduced, and the whole family is unified and on the same "wavelength." Instead of sending every child off to his own room to do his own studies, gather the children and all study one topic, but at different levels. For example, while studying about baseball, each child will write his own fictional story and illustrate it. The older child will be expected to have a polished piece of work after going through the proper steps of editing, revising, etc. This will apply and test his skills in English and composition. The youngest child will probably just dictate a few lines and draw a very simple picture. He will be experiencing the pre-writing stage. Even the father, whose job necessitates being away from the home during the day, finds he can more easily participate in the family unit while he is home. The greatest benefit to this

Using the whole library as our textbook and the whole world as our curriculum...
— Jessica Hulcy
KONOS Curriculum

teaching method could be that it brings the family back together.

While this method takes longer to prepare for versus simply laying out a worksheet or textbook in front of your child, the overuse of the workbooks and textbooks usually leads to frustration on the part of the student and the teacher. For this reason, time spent in *preparation* is much more rewarding than time spent in *frustration*. Also, you must consider the fact that this method will aid the child in retaining the information rather than having to take the time at a later date to relearn it. For a thorough presentation of teaching via unit studies, I highly recommend **KONOS: Creating the Balance** video series. Most of these concepts are presented in great detail. This 7-hour seminar is $150.00 or you can contact your area representative and arrange for a group presentation ($15.00 per attendee). Contact KONOS, Inc. for the representative nearest you.

Many parents like this integrated approach, but fear they won't be teaching the appropriate subjects at the appropriate times, especially for annual testing performance. First of all, most standardized tests are only concerned with the basic skills (reading, writing, and arithmetic) which you will most likely be supplementing with other curricula and teaching in a sequential manner. On the other hand, all the subjects aside from the 3 R's can be taught in any sequence you like. Does it really matter if bees are studied in second grade, fourth grade, or sixth grade? I vividly remember administering the social studies and science portions of a standardized achievement test to our oldest son, Tim, when he was in the 5th grade. Up until that point he had tested with our homeschool group on just the typical language arts and math portions of the test. The only reason he was tested in social studies and science was because his mommy (me) was the test supervisor and had access to the tests. But, the real reason he was tested was two-fold. First, I had become a bit fearful that possibly my lack of teaching in the "normal" sequence and (horrors) from a unit study curriculum, rather than a textbook, I may be setting my child back. Secondly, I also hoped to prove those two myths false.

Tim scored above the tenth grade level in science and above the ninth grade level in social studies. He actually scored higher in these areas than he did on many of the basic skills in language and math. Why? I'm sure it had a lot to do with the enjoyment he had with our hands-on, activity-based curriculum which gives the advantage of retention, along with the application of material through integration. But of most importance is the fact that our son had learned how to reason and think rather than just learn rote facts. There were many items on the test that I know we hadn't "covered" and when I asked how he knew the answer he said he just picked the one that made the most sense. In other words, he had learned how to apply logical deduction, a skill he practiced often and naturally as a result of reading widely about a topic and then analyzing, synthesizing, and drawing his own conclusions.

However, some parents have legitimate reasons for following a scope and sequence, such as imminent school reentry. Perhaps you simply want to be aware of this information. You can obtain your school district's typical course of study and program objectives by contacting your school board offices, a local school, or your state Department of Education. If you have difficulty locating this information, you can purchase one from the World Book Encyclopedia Company for about 50¢. The name of it is *Typical Course of Study: Kindergarten Through Grade 12*. Also available from KONOS, Inc. is a handbook containing a scope and sequence, a typical course of study, and a math and language skills checklist. Request the handbook called *KONOS Compass* ($20.00). This is particularly helpful to those who are using the *KONOS Curriculum* (see Appendix B). Another helpful book is *What Your Child Needs to Know When*, by Robin Scarlata for K - 8 ($15.95).

RECOMMENDED RESOURCES

For those of you who don't feel creative enough to develop your own unit studies curriculum, or for those who just plain don't have the time, you might want to consider using one which is already prepared for your use. Consider your family's goals and choose the one that fits your needs. One reason we chose *KONOS* was because we found that its emphasis on godly character was useful in helping us meet one of our family goals. The following is a list of available resources regarding unit studies. "General availability" indicates that the material is available through a wide variety of homeschool mail-order catalogs. See Appendix B for the contact information.

KONOS Curriculum, by Carole Thaxton and Jessica Hulcy
Available through KONOS Curriculum, Inc.
Cost: Volumes 1-3; $85.00 per volume including lesson guides.
Grades: K - 8th

> Each volume (between 400-750 pages each) is a two to three year curriculum to be used with all of your children. Each volume incorporates hands-on activities and integrates history, geography, government, civics, sciences, health and safety, art, music, literature, P.E., practical living, reasoning, Bible, and character building. Library books, including great literature, are used as "textbooks." Resource lists are included with each unit. The authors took what they wanted their children to know (academics) and designed it around what they wanted them to be (character). Activities for applying math, grammar, and phonics are also included, but KONOS does not teach these basic skills. You will need to supplement with curricula of your choice. Timelines and other materials are also available at additional costs.

KONOS History of the World
Year One: The Ancient World and ***Year Two: The Medieval World,***
by Sarah Rose, Jessica Hulcy, and Carole Thaxton
Available through KONOS Curriculum, Inc.
Cost: $150 each, Includes 300+ page student book, Teacher Guide and Timeline/Map packet.
Grades: 9-12 (Can be used by slightly younger students too.)

> A high school hands-on curriculum featuring solid academics and accurate history from a Christian worldview. This is a prepared, yet student-directed curriculum which includes credit for one academic year of history, art, Bible and English. You supplement science and math. Designed for college bound or non-college bound. Within the framework the student learns goal setting, record-keeping, organizing, scheduling, and journaling. Heavy emphasis is placed on dialogue between the student and the parent. The teacher guides lead you in developing these dialogues.

KONOS Helps Magazine, edited by Katherine von Duyke
429 Lewisville Rd., New London, PA 19360
Cost: $22.50 for 9 issues per school year
> Complements the *KONOS Curriculum* with encouraging helps
> and tips, plus includes articles by other *KONOS* users present-
> ing the specifics on how they taught a unit. Each issue fol-
> lows a particular theme or unit from *KONOS*.

How to Create Your Own Unit Studies and *Unit Studies Idea Book*,
by Valerie Bendt
General availability or Common Sense Press
Cost: $15.00 and $12.00 respectively
> A do-it-yourself guide to design your own unit studies which
> are literature based rather than a large amount of hands-on
> activities.

Success with Unit Studies, by Valerie Bendt
General availability or Common Sense Press
Cost: $16.00
> A sequel to *How to Create Your Own Unit Studies*. Valerie de-
> fines and reviews what she calls the 5 R's of unit studies: re-
> search, reading, writing, recording, and reporting.

Guides to History and *Science Scope*, by Kathryn Stout
General availability or Design-A-Study
Cost: $9.00 and $15.00 respectively
Grades: 1st - 12th
> A good "skeleton" form of how to teach history and science
> with the integrated approach. Gives general question and ac-
> tivity guides that you would apply to any history or science
> topic. Gives limited activities for specific topics.

Far Above Rubies, by Linda Coats and Robin Scarlata
General availability and Family Christian Academy
Cost: $54.95 / Companion - $25.95 / Lesson Plans 4 Vol. $25.95
> A four year unit study for high school girls based on Proverbs
> 31. Focuses on preparing your daughters to become godly
> wives and mothers. It emphasizes motherhood over a career.

This is a general high school education. College bound should plan on completing this early (perhaps 10th grade) and cover college prep courses in 11th and 12th.

Listen My Son, by Linda Bullock
General availability
Cost: $55.00
A four year unit study for high school boys based on Proverbs 3. Trains young men in godly character, Christian family life, and practical skills. Math must be supplemented and the college bound will need foreign language and higher sciences.

THE CHARLOTTE MASON METHOD

Charlotte Mason was a British educator who lived from 1842 - 1923. She was largely home educated as a child and subsequently dedicated her life to education. She is often referred to as the "founder of the homeschooling movement" since she assisted many British homeschools through correspondence. Her detailed writings revealed the deep concerns she had about the conventional methods of education. She believed in respecting the personhood of a child and instead of force feeding them information, she allowed them to read the best books and come to conclusions on their own. She emphasized "whole" and "living" books. A child would read a "whole" book by an author rather than a selected reading in an anthology to fully understand what the author had to offer. "Living" books would include biographies or historical novels. This type of book allows the reader to identify with and understand the personal lives of the characters while gleaning important facts rather than using the textbook style of rote memorization of facts.

Charlotte Mason believed in a structured morning of basic academics and then dedicating the rest of the day to real-life situations possibly through play, exploration, nature walks, visits to the museum, and reading. This would allow education to be a life-enriching, joyous experience, and adventure. She is well-known for her learning tool called "narration." The child is required to listen intently to a reading and then retell it as closely

Children benefit from working steadily through a well-chosen book... they become acquainted with its flow and its use of language. They are students of another person - the author.
— Susan Schaeffer Macaulay,
For the Children's Sake

as he can. She believed this helped a child to react with the material in an original way and to assimilate and connect information in the process. She felt it was important that children be exposed to only the best literature rather than "twaddle" which was how she defined literature written "down" to a child's level.

Mason had a strong, personal belief in God and promoted a Christian worldview in her students. Her motto was, *Education is an atmosphere, a discipline, a life*. Her educational methods and beliefs were largely resurrected by Susan Schaeffer Macaulay and then Karen Andreola.

No doubt you have probably gathered (by the many margin quotes featuring Charlotte Mason) that this is also a favored part of our learning lifestyle.

> Education is an
> atmosphere,
> a discipline,
> a life.
> — Charlotte Mason

RECOMMENDED RESOURCES

For the Children's Sake, by Susan Schaeffer Macaulay (1984).
General availability
Cost: $8.99
> The best consolidation of Charlotte Mason's writings. It is a must read!

Books Children Love, by Elizabeth Wilson
General availability
Cost: $13.95
> A listing of literature which falls under the category of "living books."

Teaching Children, by Diane Lopez
General availability
Cost: $12.99
> Following the Mason philosophy, this is a guide to what a child should know in grades 1 - 6.

The Original Home Schooling Series, by Charlotte Mason
General availability
Cost: $49.95

continued on following page

A Charlotte Mason Companion by Karen Andreola
General Availability
Cost: $18.95
   Karen's personal reflections on the gentle art of learning.

Parent's Review Magazine, edited by Karen Andreola
P.O. Box 936, Elkton, MD 21922-0936
   The original "Parent's Review" was edited by Charlotte Mason and ran from 1890 until 1960 despite the passing away of Mason in 1923. Great Britain made these available to Karen to reprint articles. The current version of PR also includes articles from families who are presently using the Mason method.

THE PRINCIPLE APPROACH METHOD

   The Principle Approach emphasizes our Christian national heritage. It stresses the belief that our nation was providentially utilized to spread Christianity westward. It also stresses the importance of knowing our Christian heritage and living according to the Biblical principles which our founding fathers modeled. Proponents consider this a way of living their lives on a daily basis rather than simply a method of educating students. The Principle Approach puts the responsibility on the student to discover and apply knowledge to his life.
   The use of notebooks to record the following 4 R's is applied to any subject. The students learn to *research* the Biblical truths of each subject. They then learn to *reason* and *relate* these truths to their individual lives. The student is then taught to *record* these individual applications in notebooks, to leave a record of what they've learned, similar to what our founding fathers left for us.

RECOMMENDED RESOURCES

A Guide to American Christian Education for the Home and School: The Principle Approach, by James B. Rose
General availability or American Christian History Institute
Cost: $39.00 Hardbound
   This one book explains all of this method from its philosophy

to a subject-by-subject analysis in light of the Principle Approach.

Bible Truths for School Subjects, by Ruth Haycock
General availability
Cost: $50.00   Hardbound
   Lists scriptures and explanations on what the Bible says about all school subjects.

Foundation for American Christian Education - F.A.C.E
Free Catalog
   Much of the available material on the Principle Approach is authored and sold by this company.

THE CLASSICAL METHOD

The Classical method of education is based on a teaching model used during the Middle Ages. The person responsible for suggesting this to be tried in education was Dorothy Sayers. She was a British graduate of Oxford University who read her paper entitled, "The Lost Tools of Learning" to the University community in 1947. It was a treatise on how she felt the educational system was failing the pupil by failing to teach him how to think. "They learn everything except the art of learning," she stated.

She proposed that the "Medieval Syllabus" held the answers to the discipline required to teach pupils how to learn. These tools for learning were called "The Trivium." The Trivium is divided into three parts: grammar, dialectic, and rhetoric. These three parts are introduced at progressive levels of maturity.

The "Grammar" stage includes the study of a language (typically Latin) and learning the fundamental facts of each subject. Emphasis is on the development of memorization, observation, and listening skills. This takes place during grades K - 5.

The "Dialectic" (logic) stage deals with the pupil in grades 6 - 8 and capitalizes on his natural tendency to argue and debate. The educator teaches him how to logically debate and draw conclusions which are supported by facts to enable him to recognize contradictions to the truth. Most students will now add

Greek and Hebrew to their language studies along with higher math and theology.

In grades 9 - 12 the "Rhetoric" stage is studied. During this stage the pupil is taught how to clearly and persuasively express the grammar and logic of each subject in both the written and oral mediums. Another important emphasis is on reading great classic literature.

Many private Christian schools and Christian home educators have taken the basis of this method and made it Christ-centered. The goal is not only to develop believers in Christ, but also to equip believers with the tools to give a logical account of why they believe, when their faith is met with a challenge. This is done by encouraging the pupils to question and dispute biblical issues of concern to them and then draw conclusions based on a breadth of knowledge. Dorothy Sayers would undoubtedly applaud their efforts since she criticized modern educators in this manner: *They are doing for their pupils the work which the pupils themselves ought to do. For the sole end of education is simply this: to teach men how to learn for themselves; and whatever instruction fails to do this is effort spent in vain.*

RECOMMENDED RESOURCES

Recovering the Lost Tools of Learning, by Doug Wilson (1991)
General availability
Cost: $12.99

> Defines the problems with public education and his solution of teaching from a Christ-centered, Classical approach. He describes the Classical school he helped found in Idaho. An appendix offers samples of their school's curriculum materials and typical course of study. This is the Classical Approach as it relates to the private school.

Designing Your Own Classical Curriculum: A Guide to Catholic Home Education, by Laura Berquist
General availability
Cost: $11.95

> A subject-by-subject and grade-by-grade guide with suggested

curriculum titles and books that are readily available today. This could save a lot of planning time. For non-Catholics: Laura lists the Catholic resources separately so it would be very easy to separate what you don't want to use.

Teaching the Trivium Magazine
Trivium Pursuit, 139 Colorado St., Ste 168, Muscatine, IA 52761, (309) 537-3641, http://www.muscanet.com/~trivium
Features articles regarding the Classical Approach as it relates to the homeschool.

CHAPTER THREE

——•——

THE LEARNING LIFESTYLE —
THE HEART OF THE HOMESCHOOL

You may be wondering why the Learning Lifestyle didn't appear in the line-up of methods in the previous chapter and why it has received the honor of being placed in a chapter all its own. The purpose is to set it apart from the methods, in order to emphasize a foundational point; the Learning Lifestyle is exactly what it claims to be — a lifestyle, not a method.

Why is the Learning Lifestyle not a method? Webster's *Seventh New Collegiate Dictionary* defines a method as "a systematic plan followed in presenting material for instruction and implies an orderly, logical, effective arrangement, usually in steps." Discipline, order, logic, and systematic plans all have an appropriate place in our homeschools. There is nothing inherently wrong with methods. The problem lies in our obsessive tendency to follow them so rigidly that we focus on the details of the method (and its curriculum) and lose the heart of the child. Instead of meeting the needs of the child we seek to meet the demands of the curriculum even when the child's resistance is obvious. More often than not, the result is sheer frustration for mother and child.

During the last few years I have talked with numerous veteran home educators who have become increasingly discouraged with their homeschools. They all mention similar feelings of dryness, staleness, boredom, lack of motivation (parent and student), and a general feeling of defeat. I was among the ranks of the discontented crying out to God, "There has to be a better way! Please show me!" God was faithful, as He always is, to gently nudge me toward the "method" I had been seeking all

> For the sole end
> of education is
> simply this:
> to teach men
> how to learn for
> themselves;
> and whatever
> instruction fails
> to do this is
> effort spent
> in vain.
>
> — Dorothy Sayers

along. The secret is that learning doesn't follow a method, per se, but rather it is a lifestyle — *a learning through the living of life.* The relief is felt in the realization that the whole of learning does not rest on our paltry attempts at lesson plans and curriculum, and that learning happens in spite of ourselves and all of our attempts to supply our homeschool with just the right books, charts, desks, and chalkboards. To be sure, there is structure and order in the Learning Lifestyle but there is far more flexibility to follow the natural flow and priorities of life in which the child's interests and giftings are capitalized upon to teach the tools of learning. And there lies the focus... *the sole end of education is simply this: to teach men how to learn for themselves; and whatever instruction fails to do this is effort spent in vain.* (Remember Dorothy Sayers of the Classical Approach?)

So just what is the Learning Lifestyle? I will attempt to define it, although by its very nature I believe it must be left open-ended since it is an individual family approach to learning. I would not want to assign rigid techniques or regimens or do's and don'ts, but a frame of reference is important. The following distinctives will help define the Learning Lifestyle.

DISTINCTIVES OF THE LEARNING LIFESTYLE

HOMESCHOOLING IS A LIFESTYLE

A homeschool Learning Lifestyle does not seek to consistently compartmentalize education and relegate it to a particular room in the house, on particular days of the week, during particular hours of the day. Your homeschool should be considered a "lifestyle," a part of your everyday experiences: something to look forward to with wonder and excitement rather than something to dread.

SELF-EDUCATION THROUGH UNITS

The Learning Lifestyle seeks to train the child in *self-education.* Indeed that should be the goal of any method of education. One distinctive, however, is that the Learning Lifestyle encourages the child to choose topics (units) of interest and/or topics that he feels he needs to know about. These could be called

> And these words which I am commanding you today, shall be on your heart; and you shall teach them diligently to your sons, and shall talk of them when you sit in your house and when you walk by the way and when you lie down and when you rise up.
> — Deut. 6:6-7

student-directed and interest-based units. Many times these are not as much "planned" as they are the natural playing out of life and its happenings. These "units" become a catalyst to teaching HOW to learn. Operating in this fashion produces self-starters and independent thinkers.

NECESSARY STRUCTURE

Training the child toward self-education requires the participation of the parent. A caring parent understands the importance of discipline, structure, schedules, and boundaries in a child's life. Therefore, the Learning Lifestyle does not recommend or promote total educational liberty as this would lead to self-centeredness and self-indulgence. The balance must be struck between time spent in individual interests to spark motivation to learn, time spent learning basic academics, and time spent in mutual cooperation between family members. This could include family devotionals, family chores, whole family unit studies, gardening together, a cottage industry, etc.

Some of you may think the term, *self-education*, sounds too child-centered. I struggled with whether or not I should use the term *guided self-education* instead. While that term expresses the correct idea of the parent being available as a resource, I fear it may also imply too much parental involvement. Obviously, the younger the child, the more guidance they will need. As they mature in this area, they will need less and less input until eventually, you can leave them on their own, unless your direction is requested. There are plenty of opportunities to directly teach our children. However, when we allow them to pursue a student-directed, interest-based unit, we need to keep out of it. It is so tempting to get into the middle of their projects and make sure they get every possible bit of knowledge they can. I agree with Jessica Hulcy when she suggests parents ought to wear a gag and handcuffs so we stay out and let them learn through discovery. So, at the risk of sounding too child-centered, I have chosen to stick with the term, *self-education*. Now when you come across it, you will understand exactly what I mean (I hope!).

Necessary Academics

As a parent, you know the body of knowledge that is vital for the future happiness and well-being of your child. Therefore, you must be responsible to introduce that information as the child exhibits readiness. For example, your child must, at some point, be able to read. Consequently, you must either make the material available so it can be self-taught (as some children are capable of doing) or, as is more often the case, you must teach it yourself. Your high school children will need to know basic financial concepts to be able to balance a checkbook, buy a house, support a family, etc. These are things the parents should teach their children whether or not it is of interest to their children. It is definitely something they will need to know whether they like it or not. Training in specific religious beliefs and godly character is important to many homeschooling families. Every family has priority information that it wants to make sure its children are founded in before they leave the home. That is what makes the Learning Lifestyle unique to each family. It becomes your heritage… your legacy.

Parental Models of Learning

We must be *models* of the Learning Lifestyle. It is extremely important that our children see us as learners and not just as the educators. To develop a desire within our children to be life-long learners, they need to see learning as something positive, even an adventure, rather than a chore or worse, drudgery. Children automatically pick up traits, attitudes, likes and dislikes, etc. from their parents. If you model a passion for learning, then they will most likely internalize learning as valuable and worthy of pursuit.

Providing an environment rich with books and other learning resources will put the acquisition of knowledge at their fingertips. Use the library when you are short on books about a particular topic of interest. Reading aloud to your children is one of the best gifts you can give them. Not only will they observe you reading, but they get the all-important message that you value spending time with them. Our good friends Bob and Tina Farewell suggest investing in sofas rather than desks!

Make sure they also see you reading silently for pleasure whether curled up in an overstuffed chair with a cup of tea, or in

Everyone is expected to learn certain skills in order to be able to face life. Reading, math, spelling, good speech, writing, and sound handling of money are survival skills.
— Dr. Raymond and Dorothy Moore
Home Style Teaching

The most valuable gift you can give your family is a good example.
— Author unknown

Children need
models more
than they need
critics.
— Joseph Joubert

But example is
better than
precept, and
more convincing
than the
soundest
reasoning.
— Charlotte Mason

bed with the pillows propped high. There should be a book shelf (or at least a book crate) in each child's room with favorite books and magazines on their enjoyment level. Create a cozy reading corner (perhaps just the bed) that will beckon them to curl up with a good book. Provide them with a reading lamp to complete the decor. In doing these things, books will always be perceived as a necessary and natural part of their personal environment.

To effectively model the Learning Lifestyle, your children need to see you in the process of learning . Right now, if you are a new homeschooler, they are most likely observing your efforts to find out everything you can about homeschooling. They'll see you reading books, going to the library, attending conventions, and seeking guidance from the experts. But don't let it stop there. I made the mistake of allowing myself to become so wrapped up in the schoolish part of our homeschool (lesson planning, chart making, portfolio obsessing, etc.) and in counselling others about homeschooling that I never had the time or the energy to pursue any of my interests. I literally put my life on hold and convinced myself that this was a necessary sacrifice for my children. The day my kids asked me, "Mom, is that all you ever do?" I realized that I had done my children a disservice. What I thought was self-sacrifice, was in fact, negligence. I had hidden an important part of me from them; maybe the best part. It was the part they could identify with; the part that is just like them… the part that longs to know new things for the sheer pleasure of knowing. They didn't know about my secret desires to nurture a garden, to stencil an armoire, to bake our bread from scratch, or to play my flute. I wasn't sharing my excitement, neither was I sharing the experiences. In short, I was not modeling a Learning Lifestyle. This realization has allowed me to joyfully pursue my interests because of the benefits to the entire family. Yes, I have to fit it in around everyone's schedule but there's a much happier mommy in this household. Have you ever seen the bumper sticker that says, "If mama ain't happy, ain't nobody happy!"?

THE ECLECTIC NATURE OF THE LEARNING LIFESTYLE

According to *Webster's Seventh New Collegiate Dictionary*, eclectic means "selecting what appears to be the best in various methods." As discussed earlier on, what is considered "the best" to me may not be "the best" to you. So, as you can see, the Learning Lifestyle leaves room for diversity.

HOW WE COMBINE THE METHODS

Jack and I believe that at the heart of the Learning Lifestyle is self-education based on interest and/or based on the need-to-know something (Unschooling Method). These interests or topics of necessity could be called units of study (Unit Study Method). Some units are student-directed, while others are parent-planned and parent-directed. Our family has grown up on the unit study approach and we love it. We still include some planned units like our ongoing American History unit out of the *KONOS Curriculum*. This is being studied by the entire family in a relaxed manner. We believe strongly in teaching our children about the Biblical principles upon which our country was founded and how to live by those standards today. Relating our discussions and readings to today's events and how they apply to us is also important (the Principle Approach). It is not uncommon for us to pursue our unit heavily for a period of time and then allow several weeks to lapse before getting back to it. It depends on what is happening in our family. Sometimes the reading of a biography or historical novel, which are "living books" (the Charlotte Mason Method), is all it takes to bring us back to a fresh look at American history.

For our young children, the Learning Lifestyle simply means plenty of time for free exploration (Mason, Moores, and Unschooling Methods). Their "self-directed units" may change daily because of their changing interests. I may never even know all the "units" my children pursue in a day, but normally they like to share with me or someone the wiggly earthworm, the cardboard house, a duck's feather, or their thoughts about a blade of grass. Children seem to have an instinctual drive to wonder and marvel at the world around them. They "need to know" about their environment and most children are not too shy to ask. Jack and I strive to "model" learning by asking thoughtful questions for the children to ponder, and then are available as a source for answers when necessary. We provide an environment rich with books and plenty of read-aloud times.

As our children mature they begin to desire the pursuit of knowledge on their own. They don't want to have to rely on us for all the answers. As they see their need to know how to read, we teach reading and writing (readiness — Delayed Academics Method). Math tends to happen naturally at first, through everyday life, which provides the concepts upon which they will build their math skills. Eventually, we turn to workbooks or textbooks (The Textbook Method) to provide drill and practice. We recognize this as their stage to learn basic facts about all the subjects (the Grammar Stage of the Classical Method). Their self-directed studies can now be coupled with journals or notebooks to record their findings and feelings about their topic and how it applies to their life (the Principle Approach).

Simultaneously, we have a pre-adolescent who is beginning to demonstrate independent thinking (a.k.a. opinionated). Although this can be frustrating at times, we mostly enjoy the fact that we can have logical (or at least semi-logical) discussions on issues of importance to her (the Dialectic Stage of the Classical Method).

All of our children, from about the age of 7 or 8 and up (or when we perceive a "readiness" for learning - Delayed Academics Approach), pursue a one-to-four hour morning schedule of the basic subjects such as reading, writing, spelling, arithmetic, and foreign language, leaving the afternoon free for their interests (Mason Method).

Meanwhile, our high schooler maintains a self-directed, goal-oriented schedule to prepare himself for his future plans. This always includes a self-directed, interest-based unit study with requirements to record information learned and principles applied (Principle Approach). This aids in fine tuning his *how-to-learn* skills. With the basic skills well in hand, we feel that the two most important areas left are polishing his communication skills through both oral and written modes (the Rhetoric Stage of the Classical Method) and firmly rooting his understanding of his Christian worldview. We want him to not only be able to give an account of his faith but to purposefully use his faith to affect the world around him.

Paramount in the Learning Lifestyle is training our children HOW to learn so they can continue to teach themselves long after they've left our home. Because learning doesn't end at graduation, we don't see the Learning Lifestyle as an approach or method, we see it as a lifestyle — because learning is a lifetime pursuit!

From this brief synopsis, you can see how we have selectively embraced principles out of each approach we feel are of most importance for our family. But, to be perfectly honest, I had never thought this through before writing this part of the book. This is just the way we homeschool. I had never consciously laid out the approaches and said, "I think I'll take this from here and that from there." I do know during the course of our homeschool years that every seminar I've attended, every book I've read, but most importantly the homeschool experiences we've shared in our family (victories and defeats) have all synthesized in such a way as to make our homeschool lifestyle unique and enjoyable.

With this in mind, it is important for the beginning homeschooler to understand that it will take time to develop your family's own learning lifestyle. The Learning Lifestyle grows, deepens, and matures, and only comes from time and experience. When you read our family's accounts, or when you walk into a huge homeschool convention, or when you hear a fabulous homeschool speaker, keep in mind that all of the "veterans" have survived their own set of victories and defeats. It is through the successes and failures that each family's learning lifestyle is refined and developed. Indeed, it is something that will continue to be refined for the duration of our homeschooling years. So instead of feeling intimidated, take comfort in the fact that, with time, your family too will reflect the refinement of your years of experience.

The most precious thing a human being has to give is time.
— Edith Schaeffer, *L'Abri*

LEARNING LIFESTYLE EXAMPLES

If a picture is worth a thousand words, how much is a word picture worth? Perhaps some living examples will aid your understanding of the Learning Lifestyle.

At the end of one summer our oldest son, Tim, and his cousin, Michael (both 15-years old at the time), spent an incredible amount of time in the two-acre field adjacent to our house. They were busy constructing a tree house that would rival the Robinson's in *Swiss Family Robinson*. (Michael had read the book the previous school year.) They scrounged wood, nails, ropes and other supplies as best they could. Eventually, we were invited out to see their masterpiece. They had built several platform levels, a retractable rope ladder entrance, a rope swing, and a 30-foot suspension bridge from one group of trees to another. Initially they relied on advice from their fathers and then found library books, catalogs, and old Boy Scout handbooks useful.

September arrived and it was all but impossible to get them to concentrate on their *studies*. My sister, Gay, and I would find them dreaming, planning, engineering new platform levels, and scheming to get back together to continue working on their tree house. As we watched their masterpiece unfold we began to realize that their "play" had become their "work"— their living education. They were incorporating math, reading, creative thinking, critical thinking skills, economics, research and referencing, practical work skills, physical education, cooperation, wood shop, biology and chemistry (Tim had taken biology and chemistry via textbook and tutored labs the two years prior) and many more learning skills into their joint effort. And, most importantly, they were loving it!

By Christmas break they were working on it full time again. Reluctantly, we decided to try an experiment. We posed this question: "If you could study any subject what would it be?" It took all of about 3 seconds for them to blurt out, "Wilderness Survival Skills!" They were ecstatic! They couldn't believe we were going to let them do this — have fun! With their input we devised a plan for the rest of the school year which allowed them to totally throw themselves into the subject. They would do library research, read, journal their experiences, and give an oral and written presentation at the end of the established time period. They began by going to the library to learn the new computer card catalog system to find a myriad of books on the topic. (Tim always avoided our very frustrating library computer system but now he wanted to learn it to access information that he wanted — not what I wanted him to have.) They set about reading and implementing. Through the course of the next five months they built a ground level shelter completely of Florida materials, a solar water still, a fire pit, added more levels to their above ground shelter, learned about edible plants and insects (they only taste-tested the plants), and learned how to hang climb and rappel from the highest levels of their tree house (since mountains are scarce around here). Many evenings we would find them hauling out the halogen lamp to continue working after sundown.

Their learning was infectious as we all began to learn from them and our own interests began to steer in this direction. All the siblings had to get in on the act and try building a ground shelter. Our niece, Jennifer, and our daughter, Kimberly, constructed a shelter which was very neat and tidy and complete with natural hooks from which to hang their purses. Our plant and tree identification books were in constant use by someone, along with the book someone gave us on edible plants. The girls concocted a pine needle delicacy for us to sample. (I know why they aren't on the shelves of the local grocery store.) Eventually, their interest turned to herb gardens.

Even I caught the spark! Testing our skills at self-sufficiency seemed to be the fever. I found myself in the library checking out about 30 books on gardening (the *real* edible plants). Because of that study we still reap the benefits of having a home garden which started out with a few pots of herbs and now grows 414-square feet of all sorts of veggies. (That probably sounds small to those of you living in the country but it's large to us city folk.) We daily stand in awe of God's provision for us. Besides all the botany the children have learned, their sense of appreciation is greatly heightened when they have nurtured the plant versus selecting it off the produce rack of the grocery store.

Young people need to be affirmed… this helps motivate them to achieve, to accomplish, and to grow.
— Jay Kesler, *Ten Mistakes Parents Make With Teenagers*

Gay and Jennifer also started a large vegetable and herb garden for their family. When we began, we collaborated for hours by phone and during visits to each others' gardens. We helped each other identify pests and diseases and then think through the solutions together. We referred to any number of gardening books in our personal, rapidly-growing, gardening libraries. Kimberly has become very good at capturing and identifying the bugs and then figuring out how to get rid of them. She usually uses the "hunt and squish" method.

But, back to the boys… It is important to point out that the boys were totally self-directed in their study. They continued to do their math, but every other subject, including English, was incorporated within their unit study. They became the teachers as well as the students. We, the four parents, and all the siblings who were old enough, learned from them. My sister and I tried many things we never thought we would do such as climbing a dangling rope ladder (now that's a sight!), swinging from a rope swing (it took me 20 minutes to get up the nerve), rappelling from a 40-foot platform (thrilling), and eating some very strange items (Yuck!). A study was published in *Exploring God's World — Teacher Helper* (vol. 13, #19, February 23, 1996) called "The Hoag's Ladder of Learning" that found that the more a student actively participates in the lesson, the more of the lesson he retains. The retention level for what a student hears is only 5%, for what he sees it's 10%, echoing is 15%, reciting is 25%, discussing hops up to 60%, working on a project is 75 - 80%. But a student retains a whopping 95% of what he teaches someone else.

"O.K.! What about the struggles?" you ask. There were many! However, I suppose not the kind you are expecting me to mention. Gay and I struggled desperately with questions we posed to ourselves such as, "Is this really going to work,?" "Isn't this too easy… too much fun,?" "Are we covering all the bases,?" and "Are they really learning anything worthwhile?" Our doubts and concerns came from the educational baggage that we carried into homeschooling with us. We felt we may be too cavalier, too renegade. When others questioned our methods we'd feel like crumbling under the peer pressure (the adult variety). But, on the other hand, how refreshing and stimulating it was to see our sons enjoying their education and with little to no input or effort from us. They

Thoroughly to teach another is the best way to learn yourself.
— Tryon Edwards

met each school day with excitement rather than a sense of drudgery. Our greatest concern was wondering how this would benefit their future. How could we know? The end of the story hadn't been told yet. Should we go back to the conventional methods to play it safe? My husband, Jack, simply stated, "We know the end of *that* story. So why be afraid?" Well put!

Since their study on survival skills, I've watched Tim and Michael take numerous eager boys and girls (and adults too) into that tree house and listen with intent to their knowledge and expertise on the subject. Not a kid leaves our home without having the grand tour and usually learning how to rappel in the bargain. (Our younger children now teach their little friends how to rappel from the top of the fence.) We have also noticed that both of the boys' interests have spread to other related fields and possible career choices. They both work a part-time job with a sound and lighting production company. Their knowledge of rappelling has helped them in that job and the owner has talked of paying for them to go to a special training school to become certified in rigging. They have also entered the local Explorer program for Fire-Rescue which mentors/apprentices young people. They are being trained to ride and participate with the firefighters on rescue and fire calls. Our son, Tim, is seriously considering a career in Fire-Rescue. Michael's desire is to become a park ranger in which fire-fighting skills are necessary. These careers take the knowledge of survival skills to a new level — helping others to survive extreme circumstances. So much for our concerns about whether or not this style of learning will have any benefit for their futures.

When Tim handed me his writing assignment I found he had chosen to write a short story. To be honest, I had expected a dry rattling off of terms and procedures. I guess he thought that would be pretty boring too. What he wrote was a fictional story depicting a series of incidents that illustrated how his knowledge of survival helped him and 127 other passengers survive a plane crash in the jungles of South America. I have to say I was extremely impressed not only with his vocabulary and knowledge of survival skills but the way in which he handled writing a short story. I had feared our experiment would at least backfire in the area of English since we weren't requiring daily repetition like so many language programs insist upon. He has never enjoyed composing and it is a chore for him, but give him a topic of interest, and things obviously change. It was the best composition I've ever read from him. So much for my fears of him lagging in the 3 R's because of too much "fun." It was Tim's composition that reminded me that truly, a child's interests, set to work at play, has meaning and purpose for his life — even for a teenager.

Here is another variation of the Learning Lifestyle that may look more like "school" but was approached from a "need-to-know" basis. Last Spring Tim became very interested in a mission trip he would take during the summer. Ecuador was the destination. Off to the library for books on this country. Without any effort on my part Tim began studying just because he wanted to educate himself about the country he felt led to serve. He beefed up his study of Spanish. He wrote rough drafts, edits, revisions, and final drafts of sponsor letters, subsequent thank you's, and an "Ecuador Report" to each of his sponsors after he returned. He was required to keep financial records of contributions and to shop for necessary travel items on a limited budget. He educated all of us at the dinner table about the geography, climate, religion, and history of Ecuador. Even his 2-year-old sister could point out Ektadur (that's Ecuador in 2-year-old language) on the world map.

So what did he accomplish? Language arts, history, foreign language, geography, cultural studies, research and reference skills, public relations, computer skills, math, economics (I'm sure I'm missing a few) and that was just in preparation for the trip. The actual trip was a whole learning experience in and of itself. He experienced incredible spiritual growth, training in leadership skills and teamwork, and a close-up study of another country and culture. Tim now loves drama (he always hated the lime light) and is part of a youth drama team that performs the gospel message in our local community. As his Christian worldview is exercised at home and abroad, he is becoming more confident in the "whys" of what he believes.

Let's look for a moment at how the Learning Lifestyle is presently working itself out in the life of our 11-year-old daughter. Kimberly has always had an affinity for animals. Her latest desire has been for a pet rabbit. After acquiring permission, she immediately began researching how to care for a bunny. Since we were buying this pet from a private source she was required to wait three weeks until the rabbit was weaned. A trip to the library found Kimberly checking out four different books on the subject. Stephen, her 8-year-old brother and constant playmate, sums up what happened next with his statement of disgust, "All she ever does anymore is read her rabbit books!" This is our daughter who didn't care about reading until about 9½ years of age. This was a motivating topic for her. She was going through her research phase. She made a list of notes that she wanted to remember, comparing information and finding discrepancies which she would report to me with great concern. Discrepancies such as one author warning never to feed a rabbit cabbage leaves and another listing it as a necessary food supplement. I immediately saw this as an opportunity to teach critical thinking skills. I could have given her my opinion but my job became one of facilitator, helping her to critically think through this "dilemma" and then allow her to draw her own conclusions. Good decision making will be a vital tool for her future. I prefer to help her become comfortable with this skill by training through "trivial" matters now, rather than through the more significant issues to come with the teenage years. By the way, she decided that until she can find out why the author suggested no cabbage leaves, she will play it safe and avoid cabbage. She also said she would ask experts in our local area and compare their answers.

Based on her research, Kimberly contributed advice to her father regarding the building of the bunny hutch. She and her father spent hours together discussing and then purchasing or making just the right equipment for the new addition to our family, Bonnie the bunny. She is now practicing the character traits of diligence and responsibility as she cares for and trains her rabbit (character traits we hope won't dwindle with time). We believe the best way for character to be molded is through practical, real-life situations.

Kimberly is now teaching us many facts about rabbits simply by sharing what she is reading. While explaining breeding and cross-breeding or their habits or diet, she is cementing the information in her own brain. (Remember Hoag's Ladder of Learning - a student retains 95% of what he teaches someone else!) Taking the time to listen, ponder and discuss these issues with her not only helps her to synthesize the information but also communicates our support of her interests which in turn builds her sense of self-worth.

The benefits to this living lesson are obvious. Kimberly was self-motivated by pursuing a topic she truly wanted to study. She used all the skills necessary to learn about this new topic. She incorporated language arts, critical thinking skills, science, library skills, and research and referencing skills. The very use of these skills to access the information she desired is confirmation enough of their necessity in her life. So just what is so important about her knowing this information? Will she ever see it on a standardized achievement test? Probably not! But, is that what we are preparing her for? NO! We are much more interested in training her *how to learn* because this will be a lifetime pursuit. The study of rabbits is the vehicle that has been used in this stage of her life to help her build those skills. In a few weeks or months she will be equally passionate about something else — not necessarily because I have prepared a unit but because it is based on her own interests.

Stephen just turned eight years old and presently his greatest interest is fishing. While writing this book, the children have had the opportunity to spend several days with their Grandma and Poppy. Stephen and Kimberly spent most of their time fishing in the river out back. The children and my parents reported a very interesting thing that happened which turned into quite a "school lesson" for them all. A huge blue heron showed up the first day and landed on the opposite sea wall, approximately 30 feet away. He just stood there and stared at them. The kids noticed a change in his expression and stance every time they would catch a fish. Finally, they tried an experiment. They put the next fish they caught on their side of the sea wall and stepped back a few feet. The heron immediately took flight, landed, stabbed the fish with his spear-like beak, went back to his sea wall, swallowed the fish, and stared at the kids again. They couldn't believe it! So, they tried it again with the same results. (It's easy to catch fish there... every young fisherman's dream - and heron's too, I suppose!) Soon, neighbors on both sides of the river were watching the show.

Ole' Bluey (as they named him) became a daily visitor. My

mom and dad reported that even on the days the kids weren't there, he would sit patiently for hours. He gave the children plenty of opportunities to witness up close the feeding habits of a heron. It was better than any public television documentary. As you can imagine, the inquiries to Grandma and Poppy were numerous. We sought the help of the encyclopedia and confirmed many of the conclusions they made based purely on close observations. Since Stephen's reading level is not at the encyclopedia stage, we read the information to him.

While Stephen learned some interesting facts about herons, his most important lesson was learning *how to learn*. He employed skills such as observation, making hypotheses, researching, analyzing and synthesizing information, and then drawing conclusions. All of this was done while pursuing an interest - fishing, which serves to implant in his mind that, yes indeed, *learning can be fun!* Life carries with it enough hard lessons. Sometimes those are our best teachers. But, when learning *can* be fun — it ought to be.

Laura and Michelle (both preschoolers) thoroughly enjoy exploring the world around them. They happily flit from one activity to another. But, their greatest interest is "reading" their books. Neither one actually reads but that doesn't stop them from reading aloud to each other. They tell the stories either from memory or make up their own stories based on the pictures. We are convinced this is because of the importance we have placed on read-aloud times. Perhaps it has something to do with the 500 plus books that line one wall of their bedroom. The collection started by accident when a neighbor gave us boxes of used picture books. Her grandson had grown out of them. When I asked how she had accumulated so many, she explained how they would often buy them from swap shops and yard sales for a dime a book. What a great idea! I've added consignment shops to our source list. When I bring home new (although used) books, you'd think I had brought them a treasure chest of gold.

We also encourage their love for reading by allowing them to go to bed with books. We provide soft lighting in their room and they drift off to sleep, often cradling their stack of books like some children do with a stuffed animal. During the day the girls' choice of music is usually the audio cassettes from our *Sing, Spell,*

Now imagination.. grows by what it gets; and childhood, the age of faith, is the time for its nourishment. the children should have the joy of living in far lands, in other persons, in other times... in their storybooks.
— Charlotte Mason

Read, and Write phonics program. They are literally teaching themselves how to read. We know that reading and learning will come easily to them because of the friendship they share with their books. Our friend, Kathy von Duyke, recently referred to this as "gentle phonics" (the title of a new book she is writing). *Gentle phonics* - I like the sound of that!

DEVELOPING A LEARNING LIFESTYLE

SO, WHERE DO I START?

"Do I throw out all our books, stop teaching my children, and just let life happen?" you might ask. No! Not exactly. The answer will depend on your current standards of education. Is your family rigidly following a particular method, allowing for little creativity or are you already somewhere on this path yet feeling guilty because you've been unable to justify it as learning, since it differs from what you've always thought education was supposed to be?

If your family is in the first category and your children are spending six hours per day at a desk, developing a Learning Lifestyle attitude toward education will not be very simple. The answer for your family may be a gradual weaning away from the books and the allowance of more time for exploration and creative play. You will no doubt experience false guilt from thinking you aren't accomplishing enough. You may doubt your children are learning if they aren't producing enough paperwork or not plodding through enough pages in their textbooks. The children may have an equally difficult time with developing a learning lifestyle since creativity, thinking on their own, and responsibility for their learning is simply not as easy for some children, as is memorizing facts and then giving them back on a test. However, within time, I am confident that allowing your children the freedom to learn creatively, will open their eyes to the joy of learning through living.

I am aware that there are many who are, at some level or another, pursuing this manner of learning. Most often I find that it is the veteran who, out of frustration and desperation for a better way, falls into this almost by accident. As a Christian I see it as a God-designed blessing after having tried every other "method" our way, and they all failed. When we earnestly seek His will, His way, we are sure to find success. For the families in this category I would encourage you to press on. If you have witnessed even a sampling of the benefits to this manner of learning, I'm sure you don't need convincing. If you are still experiencing doubts, fears, or guilt, however, the following thoughts may be beneficial.

WHERE DO BOOKS FIT IN?

If you've read anything prior to this point, you've figured out that books are foundational to developing a learning lifestyle. "Whole" and "living" books are best. Charlotte Mason describes these as superior to selected readings (like textbooks provide) which are for rote memorization of facts. Whole and living books allow the reader to glean the important facts while being exposed to additional knowledge. This doesn't mean there isn't a place for textbooks and encyclopedias. We use them in our home to the degree we feel is necessary. We generally use them as supplements and resources. A *resource* is simply a reserve source of supply or support. It implies something to fall back on for support. We like to consider our resources as *props* to help us model *how to learn*.

WHERE DOES CURRICULUM FIT IN?

Curriculum is simply a course of study. Course indicates a path over which something moves, generally from point to point. Textbooks are not necessarily employed in following the course. Fortunately, God has created the human mind to wonder, think, and ponder. From the simple observation of a cocoon releasing a butterfly to the reasoning required for higher math, our children's minds naturally follow a curriculum (a course of study). The flow of wonderment and curiosity can lead their minds along a path of reason and logic regardless of the number of textbooks we use. The use of books can assist in moving from point to point or they can be abused and destroy the love for learning.

A *prepared curriculum* can be effective depending on how rigidly it is followed and how many hours are required to fulfill its demands. The greatest problem with many of these is the temptation to focus so heavily on the curriculum that the heart of the child is neglected. It is legitimate to set goals and plan a course of study, but it is essential to give preeminence to our children's God-given ability to learn. Many are the plans in the mind of a man, but it is the purpose of the Lord that will be established. Proverbs 19:21. We can make plans that frustrate us and our children, or we can make plans that provide joy in learning. Either way, the Lord's purpose will be established. Why not choose the joyful route?

WHEN DO I TEACH ACADEMICS?

From the time your child was born, you began teaching. What a joy it was to observe his daily accomplishments; each one building upon the accomplishment of the day before. Remember how, after many attempts, a chubby, flailing hand finally steadied and grasped a targeted object? Perhaps you helped him become successful by moving an object closer and steadying his hand. Soon he became so skillful he could pick lint and old Cheerios up off the floor and maneuver them into his mouth. Ugh!

Whether a newborn, a young child, a teenager, or adult we each gain knowledge by building upon a foundation of previously learned information. Dr. and Mrs. Moore refer to this as *learning hooks* — information upon which we can hang new information. Each successive link equips us for the acquisition of greater degrees of knowledge. If important links are skipped, there is the danger of frustrating the learner with ineffective information. It is ineffective because a purpose for learning the information has not yet been realized.

So, once again, the argument of *readiness* comes to the fore. I think in theory, everyone agrees with it, but in practice it appears many do not follow it. Yes, we can cram information into our child's head, but if he has not yet realized its purpose in his life, remembering it becomes a frustrating and tedious task. Unfortunately, for the homeschool mom, the child's frustration is aimed at her since she is believed to be the source. Mom, in turn, is frustrated with the child because he doesn't seem to try, and round and round it goes. And so begins the unhappiness that so many feel in homeschooling.

I think the problem with readiness is in identifying it. Many of us expect it to just announce itself on some special day. Because it doesn't operate this way, we grow impatient and decide to take matters into our own hands — especially if *readiness* hasn't knocked at the front door on the same day as Kindergarten begins. The odd thing about readiness is that it doesn't make a grand appearance. The truth is, it has been happening all along, little-by-little, as links are added to the learning hooks. For instance — reading doesn't just happen one day. It is the result of bumping into language over and over again. Reading aloud, gently answering questions about letters, words, and sounds, holding a tight hand and guiding the letters that form your child's name, writing the words for your child's dictated stories, and many other experiences which take place, all serve in aiding the process toward full-fledged reading. It isn't some elusive mystery waiting to happen — it's happening right that moment and you are part of it.

When we become so impatient and pressured by what others will think we make mistakes that can be devastating for both parent and child. The answer to this dilemma is to gently persevere through the readiness-building stage and wait for formal academics until the absolute need for that knowledge becomes apparent to the child. At that point the pursuit of that knowledge becomes a priority — many times an obsessive priority. They will "go at it" almost to the exclusion of everything else. Its acquisition, though sometimes difficult, becomes a joy because there is clarity of purpose in the task. It is no longer a mere trivial pursuit of knowledge. Whether a young child desires to read to find out about her favorite topic, a teen desires to learn chemistry because he's seeking a career in medicine, or a 40-year-old woman wants to learn to garden for the sheer enjoyment, all will pursue the knowledge eagerly and even joyfully.

THE LEARNING LIFESTYLE
AND STAGES OF DEVELOPMENT

Let it be known that I do not hold a degree in "Child Development" from any university except from the "school of hard knocks" — which is located in our home. (Well, I did take a couple of courses in college while pursuing my teaching degree

20 years ago — I'm not sure I remember anything.) I have gained some insight from what I've read but mostly from what I've lived out with our children. If I had to make some generalizations about ages and the introduction of information from a Learning Lifestyle perspective, it would go something like this.

STAGE ONE: BIRTH THROUGH EIGHT YEARS OF AGE

Between birth and age eight, allow the child a tremendous amount of time to discover, explore, and imitate learning. Creative play and wonderment are the best teachers at this stage. Read-aloud as much as possible to open up the world of books to your child. Model learning and he will imitate you. Patiently answer his limitless questions and share his excitement upon each new discovery. Earlier today I was "introduced" to a frog by our daughter Michelle (3-years-old). She squealed with delight as she invited me into the yard. Her fascination was infectious! We took a short time to observe, wonder, and question. We discussed a few facts and she was soon on her way to other great explorations.

Every child loves to "play school" during this stage. Allow him the freedom to explore this, but don't interpret it as a request for the restraints of the real thing. The other day I overheard our two little girls Laura (6-years-old) and Michelle playing school. They were leafing through our junior library of American history books while discussing Benjamin Franklin and Abraham Lincoln. I was surprised they recognized their faces. It had been several months since we read these books aloud. Even at the time I didn't notice them paying much attention, however, learning hooks were obviously formed. As I passed through the room Michelle called out with great pride, "Hi Mommy! I'm reading my "cool" books!" Words beginning with "s" give her a "truggle" but I like what it implies to me.

STAGE TWO: AGES EIGHT TO FOURTEEN

Between the ages of eight and fourteen is the time when the most significant strides can be made to teach the basics. The foundation you patiently laid during the first stage will serve them well during this period. This is the stage when the Integrated Maturity Level (IML) kicks in. Dr. and Mrs. Moore explain this as the time when all the senses have matured and begin to func-

The freedom to explore at this age is crucial to the development of creativity and intelligence.
— Dr. Raymond and Dorothy Moore, *Home Grown Kids*

58

tion in a cooperative manner. The ability to learn happens easily and almost naturally. This is when you'll begin to carefully employ some learning resources. Don't make the mistake of "hitting the books" to the exclusion of continued creative exploration and play. These serve to stimulate critical thinking and logic and you don't want to lose that advantage. If allowed to pursue units of interest, the reasons for learning "the harder stuff" will make sense. There's a realization that greater degrees of knowledge will be necessary to move forward in their topic of interest.

I'll use our daughter Kimberly to illustrate this concept. When Kimberly was eight (three years ago) our family studied a prepared KONOS unit called The History of Art, Music, and Literature. (Unfortunately that unit is not currently in publication.) Kim has always had an artistic talent and enjoyed refining it during that unit. She drew several reproductions from the original artwork of Van Gogh, Durer, Matisse, and Munch. Her favorite was a flamingo, originally drawn by Audubon. A couple of weeks ago Kim (now 11) and her cousin Jennifer (14), pulled out every art book in the house. They decided they wanted to draw and sought inspiration from the masters. Jennifer has always loved Monet's art and together they began to notice the similarities to other Impressionists' work. They soon noticed the similarities in other pieces and began to crudely categorize the art by time periods. My participation included help with gathering their resources, drawing their attention to a few details, and then affirming the various conclusions they had drawn. I left the room, biting my tongue, knowing an ill-timed lecture could ruin everything.

On the same day, Kimberly came across her flamingo and began to critically compare it to Audubon's. Her mistakes were now obvious to her. She asked me to take her to the library to find a larger drawing of the original so she could try again and pay attention to detail. While in the art section, she came across some origami (paper folding) books. She hasn't redrawn the flamingo yet because she has been folding paper into every imaginable shape. To her, she is having fun folding paper. To me, she is practicing the skill of reading and following directions, ad infinitum. How much more delightful to learn through self-education than through a contrived workbook.

All of this learning was student-directed, interest-based, and thoroughly enjoyed! None of it was assigned or required. It was sparked by curiosity yet is was built upon a foundation of knowledge that was laid three years ago. This is learning through living in its purest form.

STAGE THREE: AGE FOURTEEN THROUGH ADULTHOOD

The final stage of development, from the Learning Lifestyle perspective, is from fourteen years of age through adulthood. With the basic skills and learning tools well in hand, this is the stage when we should allow our teens to spread their wings and truly learn through living. Their future goals should be the focus for their upper level academic studies and for their continued lengthy periods of creative exploration (also known as "electives" in school jargon). As they mature you will notice definite bents. Help them think these and other issues through. Be open in your conversations with each other. There is no time to waste; this is your last opportunity to relate and pass on your values before they leave the nest. Generally, dialogue happens naturally for families who have homeschooled from an early age, but I caution you to never take it for granted. The teen years can be difficult times. Keep those lines of communication open and don't avoid the tough issues. They desperately need our guidance yet, at the same time, we must respect their desire for independence.

Jack, Tim, and I recently had a conversation regarding this very thing. Tim (16-years-old) expressed his appreciation to us for allowing him to pursue his interests as they relate to his future hopes and dreams, free from the extraneous demands of a conventional high school credit system. He has set goals and pursued some academic subjects that I would not have considered necessary. He faithfully studies subjects which Jack and I feel are important for his future well-being (mostly without complaint). In addition, he expressed his gratitude for our assistance in setting goals and schedules and for holding him to a standard of excellence. Even teenagers desire boundaries to feel secure and to maintain a strong sense of self-worth. One of the best books I've read on dealing with teens is *Ten Mistakes Parents Make With Teenagers (And How To Avoid Them)*, By Jay Kesler (see Ap-

You need to spend enough time with them to allow those wonderful, growing, teaching moments to happen.
— Jay Kesler, *Ten Mistakes Parents Make With Teenagers*

pendix C). Avoiding them has been a lot better than living through them. We've enjoyed Tim's teen years so much.

As we begin to cut the apron strings, we keep in mind the delicate balance of his need for independence and his greater need for a strong relationship with us. Just as my parents remain a valuable source of counsel for both Jack and me, we want to fill that role for our children when they are grown. We appreciate being able to count on my parents for wisdom from a godly perspective as they continue to faithfully model exceptional parenting skills. Good communication is important both now and in the future because parenting doesn't end when our children leave our home.

READY, SET, GO!

Begin by cutting the basics back to the bare minimum. Consolidate as many of your children's subjects as possible and teach as many grade levels together as you can. Unit studies work well for this. Apportion a larger part of the day to creative play and self-education. If you are accustomed to having every moment of the day relegated to an assigned activity, this could be difficult for you. Hang in there! At the same time your children may not know how to act when left to learn on their own. At first they may celebrate like they've just been released from prison. When that wears off they will probably sigh, "I'm borrrrred!" After several proddings from you to, "Go have fun! Be creative!" you'll be tempted to announce, "If you can't find something to do, then I'll find something for you." (Although this statement usually works well to send them scattering toward creative endeavors.)

As hard as it may be, resist doing their thinking for them. A few suggestions to get them started is fine but the whole idea is for them to direct their studies in an area that is of interest to them. Don't allow their sighs of boredom to convince you that the Learning Lifestyle isn't for your family. Boredom is actually a catalyst to creativity. Welcome it — knowing that the sheer frustration with boredom will cause them to pursue interests they never even knew they had. If they have had a full schedule up until this point, they may not have had time to consider their

What really matters is that the parent be a cheerleader who shows enthusiastic interest in the teen's activity.
— Jay Kesler,
Ten Mistakes Parents Make With Teenagers

interests. With enough time and sufficient gratification from this way of learning, the word "bored" will soon drop from your children's vocabulary. We rarely hear the word any longer. Your children will soon be celebrating life rather than the achievement of a completed workbook.

At the point you and your children discover the freedom in learning through living, then you will have realized the simplicity of homeschooling; reducing education to its basic essentials to provide clarity of purpose in learning. Perhaps the greatest benefit you will experience is the freedom to enjoy the development of your own family's unique learning lifestyle — the very heart of your homeschool.

RECOMMENDED RESOURCES

The Successful Homeschool Family Handbook, by Dr. and Mrs. Moore
General availability
Cost: $11.00

The Moores are referred to as the "pioneers" of the homeschool movement. Although not the name they used, the Learning Lifestyle is what the Moores have talked about all these years. They have a few of their own twists. This book gives you more how-to's and examples from the lives of many families who have had success with their methods.

The Relaxed Home School, by Mary Hood
General availability and Ambleside Press
Cost: $10.95

Although Mary subscribes to the Charlotte Mason philosophy, she was very instrumental in helping me to see that allowing my children to pursue their interests would create well-educated and well-rounded children.

Home Schooling for Excellence, by David and Micki Colfax
General availability
Cost: $10.99

This book most likely belongs under the Unschooling Method but again, it confirms the fact that kids can and do pursue knowledge based on interest and thus self-motivation. How did their kids do? They are Harvard and Yale graduates!

Wisdom's Way of Learning, by Marilyn Howshall
General availability
Cost: $39.95

This is an example of a book with a similar theme and even similar terminology. Although I have only had time to peruse it, it is exciting to see how God's confirmation through several families' stories. This is a very detailed (300 pp) presentation of what Marilyn calls the Lifestyle of Learning Message. This takes you through her journey of synthesizing the approaches to find the right method for her family.

Educating the WholeHearted Child, by Clay and Sally Clarkson
General availability
Cost: $20.95

According to a review I recently read by Karen Andreola, this is another book with a similar theme. I encourage you to read from several sources to emphasize the uniqueness of the Learning Lifestyle in each family.

The Art of the Homeschool Lifestyle, by Karey Swan

This book is still in the process of being written but I mention it here so you can be on the look out for it. Karey is a kindred spirit on the issue of the Learning Lifestyle and we have spent many hours "philosophizing" about it. This promises to be a pivotal work on the issue.

CHAPTER FOUR

———◆———

GOALS, PRIORITIES AND SCHEDULES

Prior to launching out on any journey, it is essential to know where we are headed. With our final destination in mind, the plan for moving from point A to point B helps keep us on course. And for the inevitable times when we veer off and lose our way, remembering our destination can set us back on track.

The same concept is true for our homeschool journey. Even during the times of greatest frustration, remembering our goals have kept us on course. The goals we prayerfully set for our family back in 1984 are, in many ways, responsible for guiding us toward developing our family's learning lifestyle.

Our overall goals have remained the same all these years.

1. to instill godly character in our children so they are constantly being conformed to the image of Christ (Romans 8:29).

2. to give them enjoyable educational experiences so they will pursue knowledge and become lifelong lovers of learning (Proverbs 2: 1-6).

3. to teach them to reason and think on their own rather than to be imitators of others' thoughts (Proverbs 4:7).

You can see these are not specific day-to-day goals. These describe the results we would like to realize when the homeschool experience is over. Remembering *your* "big picture" goals will aid you in setting efficient yearly, weekly, and daily goals and schedules.

... the formation of character is the ultimate object of education
— Charlotte Mason

UNDERSTANDING HOW CHILDREN LEARN

Another factor in setting efficient goals and schedules is understanding how children learn. Without this information you will waste precious time floundering with curriculum and methods that are ineffective and frustrating. The following information has been compiled from studies done by various experts. See studies cited in *Home Grown Kids, The Successful Homeschool Family Handbook*, and other books by Dr. and Mrs. Raymond Moore, *Teach Your Own*, by John Holt and *The Hurried Child*, by David Elkind. Much of the following information was gleaned from the research compiled by Jessica Hulcy and Carole Thaxton, as set forth in *KONOS: Creating the Balance* video series. According to all this educational research, at least five basic factors seem to influence how children learn best:

1. Children learn best when they are **ready** to learn. This is especially true for very young children. Many educators and parents make the mistake of pushing their children into a learning situation too soon. Often a negative feeling toward learning can result and actually delay the natural desire for learning. Each child has his own learning time clock and we would be wise to listen carefully for the alarm. For some children it rings early, long, and loud. It seems you can't keep the books out of their hands. Then others have snooze alarms. Just when you think they are ready to learn, they hit their snooze button and they seem to turn off their brains for another nap. These children require patient, gentle guidance. Soon enough, the alarm will go off fast and furious and there will be no stopping them.

2. Children also learn best by **doing**. It is important for children to be able to touch and experience "education." When they are actively learning through discovery methods (figuring it out on their own even if they make mistakes), they will retain so much more because their learning has become internalized. Passive learning, the system which requires merely reading, memorizing a bunch of facts, and then mechanically filling-in-the-blanks for the test tends to produce discouragement. The

We learn wisdom from failure much more than from success. Probably he who never made a mistake never made a discovery.
— Smiles

frustration comes from either an inability to successfully "cram" facts or the realization that all the information is soon forgotten anyway. This short-term learning too soon establishes a pattern that can plague a person into adulthood.

3. Children learn best when the material is presented in respect to their educational development. This would include allowing them to see the big picture or the general idea before they are presented with a lot of specific facts and providing concrete experiences so they can later comprehend the abstract ideas. The educational developmental process also includes beginning with the understanding of basic concepts and growing into the mastery of the material. When information is presented according to the natural maturation of the individual, greater benefits result. See Chapter Three for further discussion on the developmental stages as they relate to the Learning Lifestyle.

4. Children also learn best when the new material is presented with respect to their learning style. Some children absorb information better when they read it or see it (visual learner), some soak it up better when they hear it (auditory learner), and still others require manipulating, touching, or experiencing the information in a hands-on, active manner (kinesthetic learner). Depending on the topic, many children (and adults too) find that they learn from a blending of the styles. Usually, however, you will discover a dominate style that relates best to your child. Making that discovery, however, should not result in teaching solely from the perspective of that learning style. To do this will never stretch him toward overcoming his weaknesses. Except in cases of children with severe learning difficulties, you should seek to teach with a multisensory approach. For more information on learning styles look into these books: *Learning Styles and Tools*, by Robin Scarlata ($15.95), *The Way They Learn*, by Cynthia Tobias ($10.99), *The Christian Home Educator's Curriculum Manual* (Elementary or Jr./Sr. High) by Cathy Duffy ($16.95 each).

5. Children learn better when they are allowed to spontaneously move in and out of subjects. The system of spending 50

We should teach new concepts through a child's strongest learning style and then review and practice through the other learning styles.
— Cathy Duffy, *Christian Home Educator's Curriculum Manual - Elementary Grades*

minutes on history, which is totally unrelated to 50 minutes of science, which is totally unrelated to 50 minutes of math, and so on is not a natural way to learn. Integrating subjects rather than fragmenting subjects helps a child to see the purpose for learning because it allows the child to apply the basic skills (reading, writing, and arithmetic) to "fun content" subjects like history, geography, science, health, and others. Many of you may not agree that these are "fun" subjects because you learned them via the often boring, passive method of rote memorization. Unfortunately, many parents will innocently pass down to their children this same dislike for these subjects by continuing to teach in the same manner in which they were taught.

PRIORITIES AND SCHEDULES

Planning and following schedules never ranked high on my list of favorite things to do. Yet, knowing how important structure and discipline is in the life of a child, I faithfully devised countless intricate chore charts and lessons plans. My problem was that I tended to have great expectations which usually turned into unrealistic ones. When we'd fail to meet my grand goals, I would grow frustrated and weary.

Several years ago our oldest son, Tim, saw me making yet another chore chart. I was sure this one, with its colorful cards and cute illustrations, would work. Tim blithely remarked, "Oh, I see you're making another chart for no one to follow." OUCH! He was right! It was another failure. Still aware of the importance of structure, I knew I had to adjust the way in which I set goals and devised schedules. I decided to simplify! My test for a workable plan became this; if my plan required hours of preparation time and reams of paper to devise charts, worksheets, and diagrams, then I just wouldn't do it. That decision has been a blessed relief for me and my family. I decided my priority was to spend time with them rather than with my grandiose plans and charts.

Now, that is my story but I know that many thrive on structured daily schedules. Others try it and become so discouraged

...boys and girls "Cram to pass but not to know; they do pass but they don't know." The divine curiosity which should have been an equipment for life hardly survives early schooldays.
— Charlotte Mason

and disillusioned that they burnout and fail at homeschooling altogether. It's ironic, however, that many of the "structured" moms feel discouraged because they struggle with trying to be more relaxed and less rigid while some "relaxed" moms experience guilt because they feel they should be more structured. My advice would be to find a comfortable style which conforms to your family's living style and don't be intimidated by what others are doing.

We make every effort not to allow homeschooling to dictate our family priorities. Instead we want our family priorities to dictate what will happen in our homeschool. Now, obviously, homeschooling is one of our priorities but it is mostly a lifestyle. This means that education will take place no matter what. This is not to say we throw traditional schooling to the wind, do nothing, and hope for the best. Schedules and boundaries are very important in a child's life, but we feel of equal importance, for example, is a visit to an ailing grandparent 1,500 miles away.

Some very structured homeschool parents would cringe if this predicament presented itself anytime during September - May. We found ourselves traveling to upstate New York in October under these circumstances. To afford the trip we decided to tent camp and prepare our own food. Now, I had never spent the night in a tent before. Motorhomes, Yes! Tents, NO! Of this fact my husband was unaware. It had never come up before. He, on the other hand, grew up camping. Never fear, a true "Learning Lifestyle" mom would seize this as an opportunity rather than an inconvenience (although I didn't always maintain that lofty outlook or sweet attitude.)

We began by pulling out the encyclopedias and my husband's old Boy Scout books and read about tent camping, especially in cold weather. We made lists of what we would need. Some things we bought and others were borrowed. And — off we went! We had been studying Early American History and soon would be studying the Civil War. Our route would take us right through Philadelphia and some Civil War battlefields and museums, so we decided to visit a few.

Many long hours of driving were occupied with read-aloud books (mostly biographies) I had collected on the subject. No, we didn't take our math texts or phonics programs but we did take our geography songs tape and came home with all 50 states memorized. We increased our knowledge of American History, our founding fathers, and Civil War heroes. We drove on top of mountains (foreign to us in South Florida) and visited an underground cavern. Most importantly, our trip allowed the children to connect once again with extended family who live far from us. They love to hear stories about their father as a child and how he was raised. They laughed with and loved on their grandparents. Relationships were nurtured and deepened. Those moments will be *forever memories* — a heritage for our children.

Allowing family priorities to dictate our homeschooling resulted in the building of immediate and extended family relationships and in some interesting geography, history, and geology lessons — not to mention learning the fine art of living primitively. We all had a blast! "What a field trip!" the kids exclaimed.

This is an extreme example of family priority versus homeschool structure. However, on a smaller scale, we might decide that a full day of gardening — cultivating, pruning, harvesting, and composting needs to take priority over our typical formal morning schedule. Upon inspecting the garden, we might find our veggies being eaten by bugs or taken over by weeds. We aren't about to let our investment go to waste just because all the scheduled worksheets haven't been filled in. By Saturday, the garden may be but a memory. *Today* we need to find the culprit eating our veggies, identify it, and research how to eradicate it. But, aren't those all learning skills? We will be studying science which includes botany, observations, hypotheses, comparisons, theories, and drawing conclusions. Basic chemistry is studied as we strive to raise an organic garden and become aware of the dangers of chemical pesticides, herbicides, and fertilizers. English skills are practiced as we research and reference data, and then journal our experiences along with our planting and fertilizing dates.

Learning often happens in places other than behind the school desk. As a homeschooler you have the unique opportunity to grab these teachable moments and employ practical application as a learning tool. Believe me, the children retain the knowledge, enjoy the learning experience, and sometimes even

What is a family meant to be?... I personally have always felt it is meant to be a museum of memories... —Edith Schaeffer, *What is a Family?*

think they've gotten out of school for the day. But, you and I know better!

The Goodchild Schedule

To put things into perspective I want to show you the schedule which we normally follow. I am frequently asked about it and I am including it here only to help you get an idea of how our family achieves balance between the 3 R's, and our Learning Lifestyle. This is by no means a mandate on how it should be done. This is only how one family does it. Even at that, I should point out, our schedule changes each year according to our needs such as pregnancies, new babies, toddlers, and as you've already read, according to family priorities. However, we try to follow this format fairly consistently so the children know what is expected on a daily basis. While we may homeschool in a more relaxed manner than some families, we always keep in mind that schedules, boundaries, and expectations are important in developing discipline and character in the lives of children.

In our family we have five children ages 17, 11, 8, 6, and 4 (as of 1997 birthdays). We start our day early enough so everyone can finish his formal studies before lunch. We introduce academics according to the stages of development that I presented in Chapter Three. On a typical weekday, this is what you might find happening at our house.

At seventeen, Tim works quite independently. Since he has a firm grasp on the basic skills required for learning, most of his academics revolve around his student-directed, interest-based unit topic. This serves to test and apply those skills on a daily basis. Tim generally spends about three-to-four hours on his studies in the morning. In addition to math and his unit topic, he is also studying some areas we feel are important for him to complete before he is on his own. These include economics (a financial planning course), a Christian worldview course, typing, and literature selected by us. He also spends time on the computer as he studies for the SAT. Each week Tim spends time in his apprenticeship program, our church youth group, and his very part-time job.

Kimberly is eleven and is in the stage of development where we are concentrating on basic, essential skill-building. She usually finishes with the basics in two hours or less. Afterwards, she is free to work on whatever student-directed, interest-based topic she is involved in. Simultaneously, of course, she continues to build her skills through practical application.

At eight, Stephen is beginning to make great strides in his reading. He just wasn't interested for a very long time. It is typical for boys to mature slowly in this area. Recently he has been more enthusiastic but I continue to move ahead cautiously so I don't frustrate him and defeat one of our goals (love of learning). Reading is a foundational skill necessary for learning all other subjects. We don't want to be responsible for starting him out at a disadvantage. We plan on about a half-hour for his phonics instruction. It is often extended when we get involved with the card games, songs, and other activities that our phonics program provides. Next, we spend about a half-hour on his math instruction. Stephen is then free to explore and play creatively — learning through living.

Our preschoolers, Laura and Michelle, are not required to participate in the formal academics, although in their estimation, it would be cruel and unusual punishment if we were to exclude them. They never miss Stephen's phonics lesson. I think they plan on teaching themselves how to read. That's alright with me!

Kimberly and Stephen follow this schedule three-to-four days per week. At some point after they've completed their formal academics, we spend time reading either together, independently, or to a younger child. If we are studying a prepared unit study, we typically read books pertaining to our unit and spend time in discussion. Many afternoons or evenings we like to read aloud, alternating between fiction and non-fiction. Jack always conducts our read-aloud times in the evening.

When we are studying a prepared unit, I try to dedicate at least one day a week to the hands-on activities suggested in our curriculum. Although we are involved in our unit throughout the week, striving for immersion in the topic, I set this day aside to accommodate particularly involved or messy activities. We all agree, this is the best day of the week. We don't take out the math, spelling, or phonics books. We only do hands-on activities pertaining to the unit we are working on. This is the day we might do KONOS projects such as dissecting a cow's heart while learning about the circulatory system or reproduce a Van Gogh painting while learning about the history of art. It would be the day we would all pitch in and work in the garden or make costumes for a medieval feast night or a foreign country celebration. Hands-on is often synonymous with supplies and mess, that's why I often call it our messy day. I won't complain though because this is when real learning (application) and real retention (ownership of knowledge) takes place. Once a week is what we shoot for but, more often than not, and if the topic is especially interesting, the children find their own ways to independently explore the subject more deeply on almost a daily basis. It's always a delight observing how the children extend their learning experiences into their play time. During those times, whether related to a prepared or self-directed unit, they are free to make messes (with the understanding that they must clean it up). Longing for the always, perfectly-polished home, I've bit my tongue many times when I've seen their creativity in progress. I know that creativity is seldom tidy and an ill-timed ranting and raving on my part could destroy the teachable moments.

A "once-a-week" hands-on day for our prepared unit, also works well for us when we participate in a co-op. Co-operative teaching (co-oping) typically consists of a participating group of families in which one mom teaches the school-age children one unit, for one day each week, for one month or unit. Then we rotate to the next home, a new mom, and a new unit of study. The children receive some positive social interaction and input from another adult role model with a different teaching style. Also we can observe how our children behave in a hand-picked group and then apply correction when needed. This also allows the moms who are not teaching to run errands, lesson plan, spend time with their sometimes neglected younger children or to simply relax in a nice, warm bath. The day typically runs from 9am - 3pm. The day sounds long but it goes by quickly, especially if you're the mom taking the bath! For more information on co-oping read *A Complete Guide To Successful Co-oping*, by Linda Koeser and Lori Marse, $14.95.

The fifth day of our week, usually on Friday, we either have another academic morning or maybe a review, catch-up, or clean-up day. You know all those kids' magazines you subscribe to and never have time to use? Well — that's our day for magazines, a quick spelling test, and other extra-curricular goodies.

Each day after lunch the children have their Bible/Quiet Time, complete their assigned chore for the day, and practice their instrument (if they are taking lessons). The rest of the day is free until dinner. It's interesting to note that many times their play is a reflection or extension of what we've just read about or studied in our unit. If they choose, they take this time to pursue their own interest-based unit.

Each evening we have a family devotional. Sometimes these are based on the character trait we are teaching from our curriculum, in which case we read Bible stories about the people who did or did not exhibit that trait and what the rewards or consequences were. At other times our devotionals consist of reading through a child's version of the entire Bible or following a family devotional series.

It would be a rare month that this schedule would be adhered to as rigidly as stated. For example, planning for, learning about, and packing for our camping trip became our "school" the entire week before we left. Our daughter's eagerness to learn about her new pet rabbit became a major part of her school for a few days as she researched in the library and then voraciously read on the subject. Or, a day of canoeing and fishing with Dad takes precedence over the books when we sense the need for it in our middle child's life. A day exploring in a park or playing on the beach as a family is a welcome change and a chance to build the memories that relationships are built upon. The point is, although we have a framework from which we work, we don't allow it to become an evil taskmaster and take the joy out of learning or out of spending time together as a family.

CHAPTER FIVE

CHOOSING YOUR RESOURCES
(A.K.A CURRICULUM)

Many of you may feel that putting together a course of study (curriculum) for your child is an insurmountable task. In all honesty it is a challenge to find what works best for each child. Often what worked well for Tim did not work at all for Kimberly. Frustrating? Yes! Impossible? No! The fact is that the very thing you find so frustrating will ironically present itself as a blessing when you realize you have the ability and authority to experiment with as many resources as necessary to meet your goals. How many schools will do that for Johnny? None I know of! This is the very thing that puts the control of *your child's* education into *your* hands where it should be.

Of course, some states have the authority to approve either your curriculum or your objectives before you begin your program. You can overcome problems in this area by wording your goals and objectives, and even titles, in a tentative way. For example, instead of saying, "We *will* be using XYZ math text to teach algebra this year", you might say, "This year we *plan* to use XYZ math text." This way you have not promised to use it if your well-intentioned plan bombs out. Now you can feel free to investigate other curricula. For further help in writing your objectives read *Relaxed Record Keeping*, by Mary Hood ($5.00) and/or *The Copybook!*, by Katherine von Duyke ($25.00).

So, where do you start? You must begin by setting your goals. If you don't know where you are headed, you'll be disoriented and frustrated. (See Chapter Four for direction in setting goals.) Your determination to achieve your goals will assist you in choosing your route. This will be reflected in your preferences of methods and curriculum.

Our preference is obvious — unit studies. I'll stand on my soap-box for a moment and tell you why we believe so strongly in this. Consider how God has modeled this type of teaching throughout the ages. He focuses our attention on a central theme, he orchestrates input from many sources to confirm His plan in our life, and then, through practical experiences, the lessons learned become ours for a lifetime. Likewise, when teaching via unit studies we focus on a central topic of study, we make use of resources from many subject areas, and then allow our children to apply their knowledge through practical experiences. Knowledge gained through experience becomes theirs for a lifetime.

Do you remember saying, "Why do I have to learn this? When will I ever use it?" Are your children now saying the same thing? When studying subjects separately, understanding is fragmented — incomplete. The pursuit of knowledge can become trivial and meaningless, losing the clarity of purpose in learning. Integrating subjects exposes the relationships that exist between disciplines and reveals how learning is interconnected and has application to all areas of life.

Whether you plan on using student-directed or prepared units, or a combination of both (as we do), it is important to understand that a balance must be struck between books (for teaching the basic subjects) and the unit work. You may be justifiably concerned that your children (or you) will want to spend all their time on the "fun stuff" leaving you wondering how they will learn their reading, writing and arithmetic. The key is to offer a balanced approach.

The first thing to remember in this balancing act is that the 3 R's (reading, writing, and arithmetic), can be taught by using anything from a conventional style curriculum to the methods of unschooling. Be sensitive to your child's developmental stage of learning as you select your resources (see Chapter Three for more information on developmental stages). I highly recommend Dr. Ruth Beechick's books, *The Three R's Series* - grades K-3, ($12.00), and *You Can Teach Your Child Successfully* - grades 4-8, ($14.00). You will learn a truly common-sense approach to teaching the 3 R's and beyond. I consider Dr. Beechick our modern day Charlotte Mason. She truly believes in a child's God-given abilities to learn and discourages methods that suppress their love

Don't put down book learning but don't be its slave either... show its application to worthwhile projects.
— Dr. Raymond and Dorothy Moore, *Home Style Teaching*

for learning. Unlike Charlotte Mason, Dr. Beechick's materials are easy to read and understand. She cuts to the heart of the matter and leaves out the technical jargon. In my opinion, these should be required reading for any homeschooler.

The second part to seeking a balance in teaching is unit studies. This will allow for the integration of all the other subjects (history, science, art, health, music, P.E., etc.). As you can see, the formula is simple: 3 R's + Unit Studies = An easy, balanced approach to homeschooling!

The 3 R's will be the subjects to use some drill, some rote memorization, and possibly some workbooks and textbooks. Still, try to make the learning as much hands-on and enjoyable as possible, especially for young children. (Use math games and manipulatives, phonics songs and games, etc.) Then apply what they are learning into your unit study's activities. Later in this chapter you will find teaching and resource suggestions for the 3 R's and other subject areas.

As you have probably noticed, I am emphasizing the resources for this type of teaching. This is because I believe that the Learning Lifestyle, unit-studies, and experiential learning may be foreign to a majority of you. I believe this combination provides simplicity in the often complex sea of curriculum choices. Possibly you may not even realize you have an option. I'm confident you already know how to teach workbook/textbook style because that is probably the type of schooling you experienced for 13-17 years. Weigh the advantages and disadvantages with your family in mind, and select your resources accordingly.

The following represents only a small portion of what is available to homeschoolers. The resources listed are among those materials I have used or that I have witnessed good results with in other families. It is important to remember that what works well for one family may not necessarily reap the same results in yours. This is even true for each child within the same family. To read more exhaustive compilations of what is available to homeschoolers, I recommend either Cathy Duffy's books, *The Christian Home Educator's Curriculum Manual: Elementary Grades* or *Junior/Senior High Grades* ($19.95 each) and/or Mary Pride's *Big Book of Home Learning: Volume 1 - Getting Started, Volume 2 -*

Preschool/Elementary, and *Volume 3 - Teen and College* ($25.00 each volume). These books are a directory of many types and styles of resources. The authors give a review of each with her personal thoughts. They are available through the general homeschool mail-order catalogs. See Appendix B.

The right you have to choose your child's curriculum carries with it the responsibility of choosing the correct materials. When you see all that is available, you may feel very overwhelmed and wonder how you will ever decide what to choose. One way, aside from reading books on the subject, is to ask other homeschooling families what materials they are using and how they like them. Another way is to attend a curriculum fair or convention in your area. Contact your state or local organization to find out dates and location (see Appendix A). Let me warn you it is highly probable that you will go through several types of curricula before you settle on one that works well for your family. Sometimes trial and error is the only effective means to finding the right material. This experience is not unusual, so don't become discouraged. Just think about what an advantage you have over the school system. Do you think they would change their curriculum just to suit your child's needs? Hardly!

To obtain information regarding any of the resources mentioned, see Appendix B. The suppliers are listed in alphabetical order according to the publisher's name. "General availability" indicates that the material is available through a wide variety of homeschool mail-order catalogs. Appendix B gives you the details regarding this.

TEACHING THE LANGUAGE ARTS

Language Arts are all those subjects taught to help your child become a clear and effective communicator. These include reading, reading comprehension, handwriting, spelling, vocabulary, grammar rules, language usage, composition, literature, conversation and speech, listening skills, research and study skills, punctuation, and capitalization.

READING ALOUD

I have become convinced, after all my years of homeschooling and using varied techniques, that reading aloud is the most significant thing a parent can do for a child's education. It has the ability to help teach all the language arts through exposure, discussion, and modeling. Read aloud from a variety of books that are of interest to your children. Continue this practice through high school. Vary between science, history, fiction, and classics. (Historical novels are among our favorites.) If you are teaching from the unit study method include books that relate to your unit. It's a wonderful tool not to mention the "warm fuzzies" as a perk. This will stimulate dialogue with your children, develop their listening skills, and will allow you to monitor their comprehension skills.

You might want to consider reading aloud into a cassette recorder. You can do this by yourself or as you read to your children. They can then listen to you read stories over and over or while driving in the car. If kept in good condition, these will become treasured family heirlooms for your grandchildren and beyond. Perhaps you can make copies for your safe deposit box.

I highly recommend the book by Jim Trelease called *The Read Aloud Handbook* ($12.95) You'll find it available in any library but you'll probably want to own it for the "Treasury of Read Alouds" he has listed in the back. His research and survey results pertaining to families who did and did not read aloud will amaze you. Time and time again the studies point out that the kids who were the most successful in the language arts were also those kids who were read aloud to during their preschool years and beyond. His chapter on the effects of television on children is very sobering. For Christian guides to children's literature try any of these excellent books: *Books Children Love*, by Elizabeth Wilson $13.99, *Honey For A Child's Heart* $10.99, and *Read For Your Life* (for teens) $9.99 both by Gladys Hunt. For a read-aloud resource that is related to the Principal Approach read *A Family Program For Reading Aloud*, developed by Rosalie June Slater ($12.00).

READING AND READINESS

If you feel like I felt several years ago, the thought of teaching your child to read is a frightening proposition. I wondered, should I teach vowels first or consonants? I didn't know what a digraph or a diphthong was and I really didn't care. My teaching degree is in social studies, at the secondary level (junior and senior high school) because I never wanted to have to teach a child to read, write, or do basic arithmetic. (So much for my plans.) But there is good news! As I found out, teaching reading doesn't have to be difficult and you don't even need to know all of that technical lingo.

Much of the mystery about teaching reading is solved by remembering this: **The Key to Reading is Readiness** (and patience I might add). I learned the hard way and maybe some of you can learn from my mistakes rather than by your own experience. Sadly, I didn't always heed the research nor my instincts about waiting. I was guilty of succumbing to the public school's schedule rather than the Creator's schedule.

Our oldest announced he wanted to read at six years old but he struggled and wanted to retreat. I reasoned he was being lazy so I pushed him to meet his challenge, even in spite of the tears. He learned to read early but didn't pick books up for the joy of it until I backed off and he was nine years old. As he developed his reading skills we continued to read aloud to him. We found the key to motivating a child to read is to offer books on topics of interest to the child. Now, as a teenager, Tim reads aloud to the family and his fluency and inflection continue to amaze us.

I must have a poor memory because five years later I subjected our second child to the same formal rigid system at age six. She was definitely not ready and after total frustration and tears from both of us, I backed off. When she turned nine I got nervous and I began to push again. The result was tears and frustration again. I totally dropped it but continued to read to her. We started the *American Girls Collection* six months later and she fell in love with them. She decided I wasn't reading them as often as she would like. One day she said disgustedly, "Mom, can I just read these on my own? I don't want to have to wait for you!" To my absolute surprise she did it! Three or four days later she commented with elation, "Mom, I can't believe how fast I'm reading now! I hardly have to sound out the words anymore!" Music to a homeschool mother's ears.

So, what I could have forced, prodded, shamed and turned into agony over three or four years, she, out of sheer joy, did on her own in three or four days. Now, it would be wrong to leave you with the impression that she had never read up to that point or that I had never taught her letter sounds and rules. But as I sat in wonder I thought about how she managed to accumulate enough information to begin reading fluently. She probably picked some up from our many false starts when I would "backslide" and try the newest program out on the market. I found we often had positive results with the materials when I used them for her enjoyment and watched carefully for signs of stress. Folks, it isn't so much the program as it is the child's own **readiness**. I concluded that most learning took place just by living and watching what went on around her. We would play games and simply talk about letter sounds and letter combinations and rules while reading aloud a book (mostly when she would ask me about it). Often her reading of simple *Bob Books* would give her a sense of satisfaction and boost her self-confidence. She created several of her own books by dictating the story to me. I'd write the words and she would copy in her own handwriting and then illustrate. For direction in this we used Valerie Bendt's book, *Creating Books With Children*, ($18.00). She would ask me how to spell words as she wrote thank you notes. She created mystery codes with her cousin to conceal their secrets from their older brothers. All of this and much more allowed her to "experience" language through free exploration. Eventually all of her senses matured and she put it all together to function as a reader.

Does all this sound way out of line?... an isolated case? I encourage you to read *The Successful Homeschool Family Handbook*, by Dr. Raymond and Dorothy Moore ($11.00). You'll read about the research, the statistics and the many families that have been brave enough to WAIT and the pleasing results they've experienced. You'll read about how the "Integrated Maturity Level" (the optimal age for formal learning) is normally between the ages of eight and twelve. So age nine, for our children, was not late at all. Learning can be forced before that, but why? Is it worth the frustration and negative side effects? Don't succumb to adult peer pressure.

Our third child, Stephen, is eight and on his way to becoming a reader. He realizes his need for this skill and as he requests assistance I happily oblige. He has made many attempts in the last two years and then backed off. That's O.K. Each time he's added more links to his reading "learning hook." I am sensing that his reading will soon "take off" but I refuse to interfere with this delicate timetable. I know he is right where he was created to be. The object is not to produce a child who can read as early as possible but rather to nurture a love and a desire for reading. That takes time, patience, and modeling. We are confident that as we provide a nourishing environment, Stephen and our two younger girls, will be reading right on target with their Creator's schedule and purposes. That's all that really matters!

TEACHING READING

You may be wondering what to do once it is evident your child is ready to read. Sometimes you won't have to do anything since some children can easily teach themselves. However, most children will need some practical assistance. Children attack reading in one of two ways. Most learn very easily with the phonics approach. Instruction in phonics teaches the rules that provide a decoding system. Exceptions to the rules can be frustrating at first, but they quickly learn to sound out the parts of the word they know and then figure it out by its use in context. To some children, phonics makes no sense at all and they will learn to read through the "whole word" approach. These children memorize words based on their shape and they can become fine readers. Allow them to find the method that works best for them.

If you feel you need some help with assisting your child, there are plenty of programs on the market. The majority of these use the phonetic approach. They vary substantially in price and number of components. Make your choice based on how versatile you want your resource to be. Those which provide readers, games, songs, etc. will obviously cost more. Many of

And reading is the heart of education.
— Jim Trelease,
The Read Aloud Handbook

these items can be homemade and save you money.

All phonics programs teach about the same way. The biggest difference is that some advocate teaching all the rules and letter sounds before beginning to read and others advocate teaching rules and letters sounds as they move through the reading process. We have always noticed that the latter seemed to make more sense to our children. Memorizing a bunch of meaningless rules with little or no application seemed to create little or no motivation. Once we introduced small, simple books that could be read in the first sitting with only the memorization of four letters sounds, the excitement and self-confidence could be seen in their lit-up faces.

Before you purchase any program I would recommend you invest $4.00 into a small 28-page booklet by Dr. Ruth Beechick called *A Home Start In Reading*. She describes how to teach reading in a common sense fashion and you may be able to teach reading with that book alone. At the very least it will help you understand the reading process. And certainly don't feel guilty if you go for a prepared curriculum. I use one with a multi-sensory approach that includes songs, card games, and practice workbooks to give variety and practice to my budding readers. (They especially love the games.) I modify the prepared curriculum to make it meet our needs and be a support to our method of teaching reading. I don't feel compelled in the least to follow the curriculum in its entirety.

If you refer to Dr. Beechick's book, you'll find a chart that includes the vowel and consonant sounds and those digraphs (consonant pairs that make one sound like th, ch, sh), those dipthongs (vowel pairs that make a new sound like oi, oo, ow), and then the R-controlled like sir, far, and her. (Whoever thought up names like digraph and dipthong, anyway? Dr. Beechick doesn't even bother using those terms but I thought you would like to know, or at the very least, you might be impressed that I finally learned what they mean.) By the way, the simple reading books I mentioned above are highly recommended by Dr. Beechick to supplement her booklet. They are called *Bob Books*, by Bobby Lynn Maslen. Set 1 contains short vowel words, Set 2 deals with blends and Set 3 contains long vowel words. Each set costs approximately $15.00 each. There are 12 readers in the first set and 8 in sets 2 and 3.

...for the best thought the world possesses is stored in books. We must open books to children, the best books...
— Charlotte Mason

So, where do you begin? You should begin with reading aloud to your child and discussing the fact that all those funny marks have meanings. If you follow the words with your finger this will become more apparent to him. Eventually you'll begin to point out specific letters and indicate the sound. It's always fun to start with the letter sounds in your child's name. If they can handle a pencil you might even show them how to write their name. When all of this begins to make sense and your child has a few letter sounds mastered he can tackle the first *Bob Books*.

Most programs begin by teaching the short vowel sounds along with the consonant sounds. Next, comes teaching how to blend the sounds. This can be a long and frustrating task for both you and your child. The day the word cat is read as "cat" and not "c - a - t" is the day for celebration. Try as hard as you can to conceal your frustration. This is when the tears would flow at our house. Maintain your composure and put the books away at the first sign of steam getting ready to release from your ears. If this sounds kooky to you, just wait — you obviously haven't attempted to teach anyone how to read yet.

The next step gets easier! You will continue to teach any letter sounds that haven't been accomplished and you'll begin adding letter combinations. As your child reads and runs into new combinations or words that seem to break all the rules, teach the sound or rule at that point. Occasionally, learning a particular rule is helpful. However, more often than not, an obscure rule will be forgotten but the context in which it was learned will be remembered. This will help him with other similar words. You will also teach some sight words because of their frequency of use like the words "the" and "of." There is a lot to learn in this step but before you know it, and usually when you least expect it, he is reading. Don't forget the importance of teaching him to write along with this step. It reinforces what he is learning and it helps with his spelling. Have him begin trying one sentence compositions and then work his way up. Have him dictate stories to you that he can copy, maybe a few sentences per day. He can even illustrate it and turn it into a book.

Last, but not least, provide plenty of simple reading material so your child can practice his new skill with ease and success. If you try to challenge too much, too often, it will be frustrating and he will resist reading. And, never stop reading aloud! I still read aloud to our high schooler and he still loves it!

A word about comprehension... There is no mystery concerning this. Workbooks are not required to drill in this area. To find out if your child is comprehending the material just ask him to retell the story in his own words. Can he do it? If yes, then he's comprehending. You can occasionally ask for more critical observations such as, who is the main character, what is the plot, how would you end the story (before he knows the ending), what title would you give this story and why? A book on comprehension may help you to know the right questions to ask but to require a child to fill out endless pages about a two or three paragraph entry is dull and boring and will take the life out of reading. Beware of too many literature study guides for the same reason. The prospect of having to pick apart every book that is read seems to dull the motivation for just curling up with a good book for the pure sake of pleasure.

My last piece of advice on reading and then I'll move on. It is very important for your child to see you reading for your own pleasure. Modeling is so important! To see you enjoying a good book, magazine, comics page, etc., will speak volumes to your child. To you dads... I am well aware that most men are not avid readers and this will also speak volumes to your sons. They may be getting the message that "real men don't read." Try to incorporate a father/child read aloud time, possibly before bed. Read some of the classics you always wished you had read, but never did... books like *Treasure Island* or *The Adventures of Huckleberry Finn*. Some books just lend themselves to a father's voice. (Even your little girls will love these adventure stories.) Your kids will be glad you took the time to make those memories with them and I bet you will too.

PHONICS RESOURCES

Remember to refer to Appendix B for a list of suppliers. There you will obtain the contact information for the following resources. Request their brochures or catalogs to see the details about what they offer. "General availability" indicates that the material is available through a wide variety of homeschool mail-order catalogs. Appendix B gives you the details regarding this.

A Home Start In Reading, by Dr. Ruth Beechick
General availability
Cost: $4.00
Grades: K - 3
> You'll need readers unless you create your own or use Bob Books.

The Common Sense Reading Program
General availability or Common Sense Press
Cost: $80.00
Grade: 1 (or when teaching reading)
> Prepared daily lessons based on Beechick's method.

Sing, Spell, Read, and Write
International Learning Systems of North America, Inc.
Cost: $175/set, includes a video. Components may be purchased separately (prices vary)
Grades: Pre-K - 3rd
> Provides a multi-sensory approach to reading.

Alphabet Activities
Available through Frank Schaffer
Cost: $11.99
Grades: Pre-K-2
> A unit-style supplement for any phonics program. Includes hands-on activities in art, science, math, reading and writing, movement and games, and cooking, associated with each letter.

Bob Books
General availability
Cost: $14.95 for each set (3 sets available)
Grades: K - 2
> Very useful with Dr. Beechick's book mentioned previously.

For the Love of Reading, by Valerie Bendt
General availability or Common Sense Press
Cost: $12.95
Grades: Early elementary.
   Dictated stories become their personal readers.

Workjobs, by Mary Baratta-Lorton
Available through Addison Wesley
Cost: $19.95
Grades: Pre-K - 2
   Not a full phonics program but teaches foundational skills nec-
   essary to excel in phonics; see "Preschoolers" Chapter 6; in-
   cludes language and math; all hands-on activities.

READING COMPREHENSION RESOURCES

As mentioned previously, reading comprehension is developed through reading literature. As Ruth Beechick says, "If your
child laughs at something in a book, he is comprehending it. If
he asks a question, he is thinking and comprehending. If he
sometimes chooses his own books, ... he is comprehending."

Critical Conditioning, by Kathryn Stout
Design-a-Study and General availability
Cost: $9.00
Grades: 1st - 8th (complete in one book)
   Helps you understand how to get at the heart of reading com-
   prehension.

SPELLING RESOURCES

Natural Speller, by Kathryn Stout
Design-a-Study and General availability
Cost: $22.00
Grades: 1st - 8th (complete in one book)

Megawords: Multisyllabic Words for Reading, Spelling, & Vocabulary
Available through EPS, Inc.
Cost: $7.15, student; $3.65 teacher key
Grades: 4-Adult (good for average or remedial child)

How To Teach Any Child To Spell and *Tricks of the Trade*
by Gayle Graham
General availability or Common Sense Press
Cost: *How To Teach Any Child To Spell*, $8.00
      Tricks of the Trade Student Book, $12.00
      Combo price, $18.00
Grades: 1st and up

HANDWRITING RESOURCES

Italic Handwriting Series
General availability
Cost: $5.75 per book; $5.75 for Instruction Guide (only one Instruction Manual necessary for books A-G)
Grades: K(book A) through Grade 6-Adult (book G)
Write Now! Suggested for Italic writing, high school-adult.($12.95)

A Reason For Writing
Concerned Communications and General availability
Cost: $8.99 per student book; $9.98 teacher guide for all levels
Grades: K-6 handwriting based on scripture verses; seven levels

TEACHING ENGLISH GRAMMAR AND COMPOSITION

Learning and teaching grammar can be a very tedious and frustrating task. Textbooks typically ask children to go over and over the same rules year after year. It makes much more sense to learn the rules and then apply them through composition, or better yet, learn the rules as they are applying them.

GRAMMAR AND COMPOSITION RESOURCES

A Strong Start In Language and *You Can Teach Your Child Successfully,* by Dr. Ruth Beechick
General availability or Education Services
Cost: $4.00 and $14.00 respectively
Grades: K - 3 and 4 - 8 respectively (includes all subjects)
   Common sense approach to teaching language arts.

Any Child Can Write, by Harvey Weiner
General availability
Cost: $12.95
Grades: Elementary
   Teaches the art of composition.

Comprehensive Composition, by Kathryn Stout
General Availability and Design-a-Study
Cost: $14.00
Grades: 1st - 12th (complete in one book)

Creating Books with Children, by Valerie Bendt
General availability or Common Sense Press
Cost: $18.00
Grade: All ages
   Children make their own hard-bound books!

Great Editing Adventure and *Great Explorations in Editing*
General availability and Common Sense Press
Cost: $15.00 each
Grades: GEA, 4-6 gr. GEE, 7th & up
   Editing exercises teach grammar, writing, spelling, vocabulary, synonyms with thesaurus and more.

Learning Language Arts through Literature
General availability and Common Sense Press
Cost: $18.00 - $20.00 depending on grade level
Grades: 2nd - High School
   Based on Ruth Beechick's methods.

Winston Grammar Basic and *Advanced Grammar*
The Moore Foundation and General availability
Cost: Basic Kit, $40.00; Advanced Kit, $30.00
Grades: Basic, 3rd - 6th; Advanced, 6th - 12th
   Great for learning and/or reviewing the rules; no composition.

Wordsmith: A Creative Writing Course for Young People,
Wordsmith Apprentice, and *Wordsmith Craftsman,* by J. Cheaney
General availability or Common Sense Press
Cost: *Wordsmith,* $14.00 / Teacher Guide, $5.00
       Wordsmith Apprentice, $16.00
       Wordsmith Craftsman, $14.00
Grades: *Wordsmith,* 6th - 9th grades
       Wordsmith Apprentice, 4th - 6th grades
       Wordsmith Craftsman, 10th and up

Writing Strands
National Writing Institute and General availability
Cost: $13.95 - $21.95 (7 separate levels)
Grades: 2nd - college

GRAMMAR AND COMPOSITION REFERENCE GUIDES

   One or more of the following books are great to have on hand
for instruction in composition and for all the grammatical rules.

Learning Grammar Through Writing
General availability and EPS, Inc.
Cost: $9.95
Grade: 2nd - 12th

Write Source 2000: A Guide to Writing, Thinking, and Learning
General availability
Cost: $12.95; Teacher Guide $14.95
Grade: 4th - 9th

Writer's Inc: A Guide to Writing, Thinking, and Learning
General availability
Cost: $12.95 Teacher Guide $14.95
Grade: 9th - 12th

***The Elements of Grammar*, by Margaret Shertzer**
Available through your local bookstore.
Cost: $7.00
Grade: 9 and up

***The Elements of Style*, by William Strunk and E.B. White**
Available through your local bookstore.
Cost: $5.95
Grade: 9 and up

TEACHING VOCABULARY

The study of vocabulary is simply to build new words into a child's language usage. Vocabulary is best taught through exposure to new words during unit studies or reading. "Real" or "living" books does this better than textbooks. For instance, a biography about Magellan will give exposure to new words many, many times where a few paragraphs in a text will not.

Limited use of skill building vocabulary workbooks can be beneficial in challenging the child's word usage ability, especially for compositions and standardized achievement tests. But, better yet is to teach the root words (Latin and Greek) so a student can decode just about any word in the English language.

VOCABULARY RESOURCES

English From the Roots Up
General availability
Cost: $23.95
Grades: 2 and up
Teaches vocabulary through Greek & Latin roots.

A knowledge of meanings, that is, an ample and correct vocabulary, is only arrived at in one way - by the habit of reading.
— Charlotte Mason

Rummy Roots and *More Roots*
General availability
Cost: $10.95 each pack
Grades: all grades
    Card games to teach Greek & Latin roots.

Wordly Wise
Available through EPS
Cost: Book levels A-C, $4.90, Student; $1.25, Teacher guide
Grades: 2nd - Low level 4th
Cost: Book levels 1-9, $6.35 Student; $4.75 Teacher guide
Grades: 4 - 12
    Workbook format.

TYPING RESOURCES

Type It
General availability or EPS
Cost: $10.95
Grades: 1st - 12th
    Teaches from a phonetic approach.

Touch Typing in Ten Lessons
General availability
Cost: $8.95
Grades: High School and Adults

TEACHING ARITHMETIC AND MATHEMATICS

Arithmetic is the part of mathematics that deals with real numbers and the computing of them. When you are teaching your child how to add, subtract, multiply, and divide, you are teaching arithmetic. Mathematics is the broad science of numbers, quantities, measurements, and shapes, and how they relate to each other. This includes arithmetic, algebra, geometry, calculus, and trigonometry.

While teaching math (arithmetic), especially to the young child, it is important that the abstract be taught by using concrete objects. For example, look at 2+2=4. Each figure is a symbol for an abstract object. The symbol for two (2) or a plus sign (+) or an equal sign (=) has no meaning to a young child unless he has had a chance to relate it to some concrete experience. For this reason math manipulatives are very important.

Working with manipulatives helps the child to "see" and "feel" how math works. Manipulatives can be real-life objects used during real-life activities. Setting the table with four plates, four forks, etc. or eating a whole sandwich vs. one cut in half or quarters are examples of real-life manipulatives. Some families like to extend this experience by using manufactured manipulatives such as rods, counting chips, counting links, cubes, etc. As the child develops an understanding of the underlying concepts of math through the use of manipulatives, he will begin to naturally and gradually move away from the manipulatives toward the sole use of the abstract symbols. The child's mind will be able to easily draw from his concrete experiences to aid in his work with the abstract.

Drill is also an essential part of teaching mathematics and should not be neglected. This should be done after a concept is understood to give the child the skill he needs to speed up the calculation process.

ARITHMETIC AND MATH RESOURCES

An Easy Start In Arithmetic and *You Can Teach Your Child Successfully,* by Dr. Ruth Beechick
General availability or Education Services
Cost: $4.00 and $14.00 respectively
Grades: K-3 and 4-8 respectively
Highly recommended to give you an easy and complete understanding of the concepts and how-to's of teaching math.

A bag of beans, counters, or buttons should be used in all the early arithmetic lessons, and the child should be able to work with these freely...
— Charlotte Mason

Cuisenaire Math Manipulatives

General availability and Addison-Wesley
Cost: varies
Grades: Pre-K - 12th
Provides manipulative rods and workbooks.

Family Math

General availability
Cost: $18.00
Grades: K - 12
Hands-on activities to teach many concepts.

Key to... Workbooks

General availability or Key Curriculum Press
Cost: $2.10 per workbook. Number of workbooks vary according to subject.
Grades: 4 - 12 (For average student or remedial)
Workbooks for fractions, decimals, percents, algebra, and geometry; no manipulatives

Making Math Meaningful

Cornerstone Curriculum Project or Lifetime Books and Gifts
Cost: Kindergarten: $30.00; Manipulative package: $15.00;
Grades 1st - 6th: $40.00 Alg. 1: $45.00; Geom.: $45.00
Grades: K - high school algebra and geometry
Manipulatives and worksheets; tells you exactly what to do and say; teaches concepts before calculation; no drill

Math-It Series

General availability
Cost: *Pre Math-It* and *Math-It*, $34.95; *Advanced Math-It*, $15.00;
Grades: Pre-K and up
Pre-Math-It teaches number patterns with dominoes (ages 5-7)
Math-It teaches addition, doubling, and multiplication (7-12 yrs)
Advanced Math-It teaches percentages and division (12 and up).
Great for drill work and teaching tricks to remember math facts. Limited manipulatives: dominoes for *Pre-Math-It*; gameboard and cards for *Math-It* and *Advanced Math-It*.

The chief value of arithmetic... lies in the training it affords to the reasoning powers, and in the habits of insight, readiness, accuracy, intellectual truthfulness it engenders.
— Charlotte Mason

Miquon Math
Key Curriculum Press and General availability
Cost: Teacher Manual $13.95
      Student books $5.95 each (6 levels)
Grades: 1 - 3
    Uses Cuisenaire Rods with workbooks

Saxon Math
Saxon Publishers, Inc. and General availability
Cost: $44.95 - $90.00
Grades: K - 12th
    K-3 use manipulatives heavily, 4-12 textbooks only.
    Teaches math in increments and then continual review. Considered by some to provide too many practice problems squelching any joy for learning math.

Workjobs
Available through Addison-Wesley
Cost: $19.95
Grades: K-2
    Hands-on activities to teach foundational concept skills necessary to think mathematically and excel; see Chapter Six: Preschoolers: Ages 4 and 5)

TEACHING HISTORY, GOVERNMENT, ECONOMICS AND GEOGRAPHY
(Also Known As: SOCIAL STUDIES)

In several seminars, I've taken a very unscientific survey (a show of hands) to find out how many adults ranked history as their least favorite subject. It is always well over the majority. Why is that? History is not boring. Most of those same adults confess that they enjoy biographies, historical novels, documentaries on the lives of historical figures, or travelogues of countries. So what is the reason? The method by which it was taught! Truthfully, who enjoys reading predigested information and then answering the 15 questions at the end of the chapter? I didn't!

You didn't! And, neither will your children. So what's the alternative? How about biographies, historical novels, documentaries, and travelogues, just to name a few! Don't forget that all the social studies lend themselves well to the unit studies method.

Textbooks can serve as references, but they are also a very condensed source of predetermined information. Someone else got to read all the good stuff and also did all the synthesizing, analyzing, and drawing conclusions that your children should do. How much better it is to give our children broad exposure to information through "living" or "real" books and allow them to draw their own conclusions. Your library is an easy source for these types of books. It is true that we may sometimes come across biased information or something offensive but this too can be used to strengthen our abilities to discern and reason in light of what we know to be God's underlying truths. To expose ourselves to God's underlying truths we can search out sources of information that are written from a godly perspective.

The very best way to teach this and all of the following subjects is through an integrated approach - Unit Studies. The library is a great place to find many supportive resources. The following are listed because they are worth adding to your home library. I have found them to be reliable and highly stimulating. There's no need to be bored with history any longer!

HISTORY RESOURCES

Guidelines to History, by Kathryn Stout
Design-a-Study and General availability
Cost: $9.00
Grades: 1st - 12th
   Create your own unit study with this framework that integrates all subjects with a history focus.

Let the Authors Speak: A Guide to Worthy Books
Based on Historical Setting, by Carolyn Hatcher
General availability
Cost: $18.95

continued on following page

History... should form in him, insensibly, principles whereby he will hereafter judge of the behavior of nations, and will rule his own conduct as one of a nation. This is what the study of history should do for the child.
— Charlotte Mason

A proponent of the Charlotte Mason philosophy. In particular this book leads you to the "living books" listed by century and location and then again listed by author. A resource of over 1000 books... a lifetime of reading!

Greenleaf Press Materials, by Rob and Cyndy Shearer
Greenleaf Press and General availability
Cost: Most guides are $8 - $11.00. Biographies are $16.00. Combined packages with supplemental books vary in price.
Grades: 1st - 6th
Studies history chronologically through brief biographies of famous men who lived during major eras. Guides suggest dialogue questions and activities.

The Light and the Glory and *From Sea to Shining Sea*,
by Peter Marshall and David Manuel
General availability
Cost: $12.00 each (paperback); Study Guides, $8.00 each
Grades: Jr. High - Adult. However, they have also written a children's version for each book for ages 9 - 12 ($10.00 each).
Both versions give America's history from a Christian perspective. *The Light and the Glory* covers Columbus through the American Revolution. *From Sea to Shining Sea* covers the period of westward expansion and the pioneers through pre-Civil War.

Usborne Books
EDC or General availability
Cost: varies
Grades: varies
The titles are too numerous to list. Order their catalog for a complete listing. Written from a secular viewpoint so Christians may find some entries or illustrations objectionable.

Streams of Civilization Volumes I and II
Christian Liberty Academy Press and General availability
Cost: $17 each
        Teacher Guide, $4.50 each
        Test booklet and key, $3.50 each
Grades: 6th - 10th

One of the few examples of a textbook (hardbound) which is a great read and reference book. Written from a Christian perspective. Volume I covers ancient civilization to pre-1600. Volume II covers the Reformation through present day.

America, The First 350 Years, by Steven Wilkins
General availability
Cost: $69.95 for 16 audio cassette tapes and a 200-page binder of lecture notes, study notes, and discussion questions.
Grades: Older Jr. High - Adult
A Biblical look at America's history covering Columbus through the Reconstruction in a lecture format.

GOVERNMENT RESOURCES

Remember to integrate this topic with your study of history.

God and Government Volume 1, 2, and 3, by Gary DeMar.
General availability
Cost: $12.95 each volume (paperback)
Grades: Jr. High and up
Similar to a textbook format but a great resource for those seeking a Christian perspective to the foundations of our government.

ECONOMICS RESOURCES

Remember to integrate this topic with your study of history.

Surviving the Money Jungle and *Get a Grip on Your Money*,
by Larry Burkett
General availability
Cost: $7.50 for student workbook and $9.50 for the Leader's guide
Grades: *Surviving the Money Jungle* is Jr. High level
Get a Grip on Your Money is High School
Teaches young people how to manage their money. Written from a Christian perspective.

Whatever Happened to Penny Candy, by Richard Maybury
General availability
Cost: $9.95 and the teacher's guide is 95¢
Grades: Jr. High and up
> Format is a young man writing questions about economics to his Uncle Eric. He provides the answers in this easy to read and stimulating book.

GEOGRAPHY RESOURCES

Remember to integrate this topic with your study of history.

Sing Around the World Geography Tapes, by Larry and Kathy Troxel
General availability
Cost: $19.95 Kit includes 1 cassette with 18 songs, a world map, and a 96 page workbook with lyrics, maps, and puzzles.
Grades: elementary and up
> This is what our family used to memorize all the states and their locations on the map.

Hands On Geography, by Maggie Hogan and Janice Baker.
General availability
Cost: $14.95
Grades: elementary
> An activity-oriented approach to geography

Mapping the World By Heart, by David Smith
General availability
Cost: $59.95
Grades: 5th - 12th
> Includes video, notebook, and reproducible maps. Through hands-on activities children are eventually able to draw maps of the continents without the aid of a prepared map.

Operation World, by Patrick Johnstone
General availability
Cost: $12.99

Grades: Written at a high school and above reading level, but most families use it together to study countries and then pray for the needs that are listed.

You Can Change Your World, by Jill Johnstone
General availability
Cost: $14.99 (Hardbound)
Grades: Elementary
This is a children's version of the above book. We've used both for our family devotions. Our big world map becomes an integral part of our evening.

TEACHING SCIENCE

The term "science" actually means the accumulation of knowledge, especially the knowledge attained through the study or practice of something. In other words, we are trying to get our questions answered. In an educational sense, when we speak of the subject "science," we are referring to the study of natural science like the earth, life, and physical sciences.

So, how do we go about making this pursuit of knowledge about natural science interesting and desirable to our children? How about if we concentrate on the word "natural." Children tend to just "naturally" or instinctively enjoy observing, collecting, and pondering nature. Young children need to be able to have a lot of freedom to explore and enjoy God's creation without a lot of interference and forced terminology like hypothesis, variables, data, and so forth. Exposure to these terms in an incidental way is appropriate but never to the point of disdain. It is also appropriate for you to familiarize yourself with the terminology and scientific method of testing hypotheses so you can gently guide your children into this as they mature. This subject is best taught through the unit study/integrated method of learning.

When is the right time to introduce the formal study of science? Your children will be the best indicators. Eventually the questions they ask will become so sophisticated it will be "natural" to pursue a deeper study of the topic they are pondering. Remember that the more hands-on and experiential you make

Nature is the art of God.
— Dante

the instruction, the more they will enjoy and retain the information. Older students may find the textbooks of upper level science courses beneficial, but don't forget to include the labs. That's what keeps it experiential and exciting. If you don't feel you can adequately teach these subjects, you can do as we did. We found a former biology and chemistry teacher to give lab classes to a small group of homeschoolers in our community since none of us felt qualified, nor had the proper equipment.

If you are interested in teaching "Creation Science" I have included some popular and helpful resources.

SCIENCE RESOURCES

Science Scope, by Kathryn Stout
Design-a-Study and General availability
Cost: $15.00
Grades: Kindergarten - 12th
Orients you to scientific terminology, the necessary skills, topics, and concepts for each grade level, and then explains HOW to teach it all. Great for unit studies.

The Usborne Illustrated Dictionary of Science: Physics, Chemistry, and Biology Facts
EDC or General availability
Cost: $23.95
Grades: Jr. High and up

Science Fair Manual, by Kim Harthun
General availability or Kim Harthun
Cost: $6.50
Grades: all levels
Teaches all aspects of preparing a project for a Science Fair

The Backyard Scientist, by Jane Hoffman
General availability or Backyard Scientist
Cost: $8.50 each book
Clearly written instructions to perform experiments with

If a child is to keep alive his inborn sense of wonder, he needs the companionship of at least one adult who can share it, rediscovering with him the joy, excitement and mystery of the world we live in.
— Rachel Carson (1907-1964) American biologist

household products. Experiments involve chemistry, physics, and biology related topics.

Lab Science: The How, Why, What, When, Who, 'n' Where Book,
by Barb Shelton
General availability or Homeschooling Seminars and Publications
Cost: $11.95
  A manual with reproducible forms to help you teach science labs to your high schooler.

Nature's Friend
P.O. Box 22777 SR 119, Goshen, IN 46526 / (219) 534-2245
Cost: $22.00/annual subscription. Arrives monthly.
  Nature articles with Christian perspective for ages 4 - 13.

Tobin's Lab Catalog
P.O. Box 6503, Glendale, AZ 85312
(800) 522-4776 / (602) 843-4265
Cost: Free catalog
  This homeschool family carries a huge variety of scientific equipment, chemicals, kits, reference books, charts, and much, much more! Perfect for accommodating science-related unit studies.

CREATION SCIENCE RESOURCES

Unlocking the Mysteries of Creation, by Dennis Petersen
General availability
Cost: $22.95 (hardbound)
Grades: Jr. High and up can read it on their own but it was developed for parents to read aloud and discuss with children of all ages.

Creation Science: A Study Guide to Creation,
by Felice Gerwitz and Jill Whitlock
General availability
Cost: $14.95
Grades: Kindergarten - 12th
  A prepared unit study for teaching Creation Science.

> Nature Knowledge... the most important for young children... there is no sort of knowledge to be gotten in these early years so valuable to children as that which they get for themselves of the world they live in.
> — Charlotte Mason

Dinosaurs by Design
General availability
Cost: $15.95 (hardbound)
Grades: 1st - Adult
> Explains the creation and extinction of dinosaurs. Includes colorful pictures and descriptions of dinosaurs.

It Couldn't Just Happen: Faith Building Evidences for Young People, by Lawrence Richards
General availability
Cost: $14.99
Grades: 4th - 8th
> Biblical answers to questions kids ask about creation and our world. Textbook format.

TEACHING WORK STUDY SKILLS

Work study skills are those skills that should be ranked along side the 3 R's and in my opinion, are considered survival skills for the real world. There are two categories of work study skills. The first deals with *visual materials*, regarding the ability to get and use information from maps, tables, and graphs. These are all tools for communicating vast amounts of knowledge and require specific skills and instruction to be useful. The second category of work study skills deals with the use of *reference materials*. Skills involved are using a table of contents, an index, a dictionary, encyclopedias, guide words, key words, general reference materials, and alphabetizing.

The best way to teach this is through role-modeling and real-life experiences. In my opinion, typical textbooks do not cover these topics sufficiently. When I was growing up and I would ask my mom a question she would almost always say, "Let's go look it up." There were many times I would see her sitting on the floor in front of the encyclopedia case just reading about some subject she was curious about. We would look up a word in the dictionary and 20 minutes later she would still be reading definitions of words totally unrelated. We used to laugh and tease her a bit but you know what? — this significant role model has

I think we owe it to children to let them dig their knowledge, of whatever subject, for themselves out of the fit book; and this for two reasons: What a child digs for is his own possession; what is poured into his ear... floats out as lightly as it came in, and is rarely assimilated.
— Charlotte Mason

rubbed off on her children. In our own homes and when we get together for big family functions we often find ourselves around the dinner table, pushing back the dishes and reading some entry out of the dictionary, encyclopedia, or medical journals. Mom just looks at us and smiles that "proud mother's" smile and we all know that she is glad we picked up her habit. I hope to model the same for my children.

If your children aren't getting enough real-life experiences you may find it necessary to supplement with skill builders. Many standardized tests will evaluate these areas. It is a good idea to have your child ready.

WORK STUDY SKILLS RESOURCES

Information Please!
D.P. and K. Productions and General availability
Cost: *Getting Started*, $18.00
       Beginning, Intermediate, and *Advanced*, $15.00 each level
Grades: *Beginning* (K-4), *Intermediate* (5-8), *Advanced* (9-12)
   Hands-on supplement to teach the use of reference materials by doing their own research.

Weekly Reader Skills Books
Weekly Reader Corporation
Cost: Most are $2.10 per 32 page booklet. None are over $3.00.
Grades: K - 6th
   Can be used for elementary students who have not had much previous exposure to these skills. Their workbooks for maps, tables and graphs are helpful for explanation and drill.

Teaching Children to Use the Library, by Mary Hood
General availability or Elijah Company
Cost: $5.00
   Parent resource

TEACHING COMPUTER SKILLS

Well, let's face it! We live in the computer age and like it or not, we need to have some computer literacy and so do our children, although I suppose that would be argued by some. The ownership of PC's is increasing at a phenomenal rate among homeschoolers. If you are an owner then you need to know the best of what is available. I would be crazy to try to inform you about the computer world in this book since we all know it would be outdated before it reached the publishers. Instead I will give you some resources to help you get started, get online, acquire the best available software, and sources for continually updated information.

A word of caution: I recommend limited use of the computer. If you are homeschooling so you can teach and interact with your child then only use the computer as a supplement. This piece of technology can rob your child of precious hours of creativity just as surely as the television can... maybe even more!

Another word of caution if you plan on using the internet — Beware of the negative content that is easily accessible and tempting to young minds.

The Home Computer Market: A Hardware and Software Planning Guide and Product Catalog, owned and operated by the Kihlstaiuses
Available through The Home Computer Market.
Cost: Free catalog
Grades: all levels
> This is a catalog full of information regarding the use of a PC. They sell customized computer packages and educational software. All software has been screened for wholesome content and from a Christian perspective. Yearly catalogs keep the information updated.

Homeschool PC Magazine, published by Bill and Mary Pride.
Available through Home Life
Cost: $19.95 for 6 issues (1 year) or $35 for 12 issues (2 years)
Grades: Older students and parents

An up-to-date guide to computer information and tons of reviews on educational software. Coming from a Christian perspective, Bill and Mary promise to screen all recommended software for offensive material.

Homeschool Guide to the Online World - Everything You Need to Know to Start Making Great Connections, by Mark and Wendy Dinsmore
General availability
Cost: $12.99
Grades: For all levels of computer users.

Homeschooling and the Internet and *Homeschooling and the Internet, Yellow Pages*, by Lynn Coleman
General availability
Cost: $11.95 each

> The first book is especially designed to teach the new user how to use the internet. The second book has approximately 800 internet web site addresses of interest to the homeschooler.

TEACHING THE FINE ARTS

All of the arts (music, art, drama, and dance) reflect ideas and philosophies and therefore can define a person's worldview or even an entire culture's worldview. These are the beliefs of the late Francis Schaeffer, a noted Christian philosopher of our time. During our unit study of the History of Art, Music, Literature, and Technology, we became convinced that he was absolutely correct. If we had never read any of the historian's words but only looked at the paintings and sculptures, listened to the music, and read the poetry and stories of any of the specific periods of history, we could have interpreted their prevailing belief system. If that be the case, I'm afraid our culture will leave a disappointing legacy. I can't be sure if any of our children will ever be an influence in this area but it would be less likely if we never educated them or allowed them to pursue obvious giftings. With that in mind, I feel that this often neglected area should be given a place of importance.

To me it seems as if when God conceived the world, that was poetry; He formed it, and that was sculpture; He varied and colored it, and that was painting; and then, crowning all, He peopled it with living beings, and that was the grand divine, eternal drama.
— Charlotte Cushman

If your child seems to have a special interest or gifting and if you feel unqualified to teach these skills, find those who can teach and train your child in his area of gifting. At the very least you can learn together the history of the arts and their influence on our present-day society. We were surprised at the conclusions we came to and how they have affected our own worldviews.

ART RESOURCES

Art Adventures at Home, Level 1 and 2, by Jean Soyke
General availability
Cost: $19.95 each level
Grades: Level 1 for K - 2nd, Level 2 for 3rd - 5th
   Step-by-step lesson plans with room for flexibility. Teaches the elements of art: line, shape/form, color, and texture.

Drawing With Children and *Drawing for Older Children and Teens*, by Mona Brookes
General availability
Cost: $13.95 each book
Grades: Titles explain levels
   This method assumes no prior knowledge of art and it really works! Even I learned to draw! Teaches the 5 basic shapes that combine to form all objects and then how to recognize them and draw them. Emphasizes critical observation skills which are useful for other areas of life.

KidsArt Magazine
P.O. Box 274, Mt. Shasta, CA 96067 (916) 926-5076
Cost: $10.00 per year subscription, arrives quarterly
Grades: elementary and possibly higher
   Each issue features one topic and then gives many activities with directions. Includes projects, history, and appreciation of art. This could provide a total art program.

Art is the gift of God, and must be used unto His glory. That in art is highest which aims at this.
—Michelangelo

How Should We Then Live?: The Rise and Decline of Western Thought and Culture, by Francis Schaeffer
General availability
Cost: $14.99
Grades: High School and adult
> Presents belief that a culture's ideas and philosophies are reflected in art. Shows proof of this by a study of each major culture. Emphasizes Christian worldview.

Adventures in Art, by David Quine
Available through Cornerstone Curriculum Project
Cost: Gallery 1-$60; Gallery 2 & 3-$55 each; Portfolio-$30
Grades: 1st - 12th
> Based on the teachings of Francis Schaeffer. Quality prints are provided to illustrate how art reflects ideas. Includes a discussion guide.

The National Gallery of Art - Publications Office
6th and Constitution Avenue N.W., Washington, DC 20565
(202) 842-6263
> Request their $3.50 catalog and free *Extension Programs Catalog*. We bought very inexpensive postcards of reproductions while studying art history and made our own Art History Timeline Portfolio. You can also borrow audio-visual materials for only the cost of return postage.

History of Art, by H.W. Janson (Abrams) and *History of Art for Young People*, by A.F. Janson (Prentice Hall)
Available through Lifetime Books and Gifts or Elijah Company
Cost: *History of Art*, $60, over 850 pp. Check used bookstores or library; *History of Art for Young People*, $35. (fewer illustrations)
Grades: *History of Art* for high school & adult; *History of Art for Young People* for elementary - jr. high.
> We used these two books as our major texts and for information for our timeline. They are heavily illustrated and do contain nude pictures of original art work or sculptures. Teaches the history of each culture in chronological order. The illustrations include most of the art works that Francis Schaeffer refers to in *How Should We Then Live?*.

We are created in the image of a Creator. So we are, on a finite level, people who can create.
— Edith Schaeffer, *The Hidden Art of Homemaking*

All great art is the expression of man's delight in God's work, not his own.
— Ruskin

107

MUSIC RESOURCES

Music and Moments with the Masters, compiled by David Quine
Available through Cornerstone Curriculum Project
Cost: Set 1 - $55 (cass.), $75 (CD); Set 2,3,&4 - $45 each (cass.);
$65 each (CD)
Grades: all ages
> Good way to introduce classical music. 16 composers are featured with music and biographies. The book, *The Gift of Music*, is included.

Classical Composers and the Christian World View, by David Quine
Available through Cornerstone Curriculum Project
Cost: $30 for 6 cassettes; $50 for 6 CD's
Grades: Jr. High and High School
> The continuation to *Music and Moments with the Masters* and the companion to *Adventures in Art*. Purpose is to show how worldviews are reflected in music. Provides a book with the dialogue to use with your children, as the music is studied from the Baroque to the Modern period.

The Gift of Music - Great Composers and Their Influence, by Jane Stuart Smith and Betty Carlson
General availability
Cost: $15.99
Grades: High School and Adult
> Detailed biographies of composers. Written from a Christian perspective.

DRAMA IDEAS

Drama can be simple or elaborate, spur-of-the-moment or well-planned. Although this isn't one of my great loves, the *KONOS Curriculum* taught me that dramatizing is an important tool for retention of knowledge. Throughout the years I have found this to be accurate. One evening after our devotional, the children dramatized the story we read about wise King Solomon and the bluff decision he made to cut the baby asunder. The kids ran and grabbed a plastic sword, a cardboard Burger King® crown, a bathrobe for a king's robe, and a baby doll. Voila! a dramatization! At another time we spent an entire month coordinating a medieval feast presentation for 14 children and their families, complete with costumes, food, script, music, dance, jousting, animals, and dramatic readings and recitations. The children still speak of these and other dramatic events because they stand out in their memories. Our oldest son went on a summer short-term mission trip where street drama was the witnessing vehicle. Drama was never his "thing" and we were all surprised when he was assigned the lead role. He came home excited about drama! Recently Tim attended a Civil War reenactment complete with costumes and muskets. Now he's really hooked! Even if you think you don't have a dramatic bone in your body, give it a try! I think you'll get hooked too, or at the very least be enthused by its effectiveness!

Drama Made Easy, by Karena Krull
Available through Eternal Hearts
Cost: $16.95
   A step-by-step manual for the producer or director of a play. Includes the how-to's from production through performance.

TEACHING CHILDREN WITH LEARNING DIFFICULTIES

   No doubt there are many of you struggling with a child who just doesn't seem to be learning at the same rate as his age-mates. They are often described in medical-sounding terms as having a learning disability, an attention deficit disorder, attention deficit and hyperactive disorder or dyslexia or something else along that line. The implication, despite at least average intelligence, is that their brains do not function normally.
   Many teachers and parents are too willing to accept these labels and assume that the child is doomed to a lifetime of learning difficulties. Don't fall for that!! Yes, there is a problem, but it is not in their general learning abilities but rather a problem in mastering the coding and decoding systems of the classroom

> The aim and final reason of all music should be nothing else but the glory of God and the refreshment of the spirit.
> — J.S. Bach

(whether at home or in a conventional school). The child has specific instructional needs rather than learning problems. He may learn differently than most other children but he can learn! Knowing this, we should no longer call these children learning disabled; they are simply "different learners." And, you need to be a different teacher to meet their needs. Here are a few resources to help you understand how to do that and to put you in touch with other parents who have similar concerns and challenges. There is hope and help!

Learning in Spite of Labels, by Joyce Herzog
Greenleaf Press and General availability
Cost: $9.95
Grades: For parents
Provides tips on teaching the different learner and gives a Christian perspective of education.

Choosing and Using Curriculum for Your Special Child, by Joyce Herzog
Greenleaf Press and General availability
Cost: $9.95
Grades: For parents
Includes reviews of hundreds of curriculum programs for the special needs child.

Learning Power: Helping Children Reach Their Potential, by Nancy Hellwege
Available through Learning Power
Cost: $35.00
Grades: Parent resources
Covers techniques to improve math, reading, writing, grammar, and spelling. Loaded with activities.

Developing Your Child For Success, by Kenneth Lane
Available through Learning Potentials Publishing
Cost: $24.95
Grades: For parents to use with ages 4 and up
System develops perceptual abilities, visual memory, eye-hand coordination, motor skills, visual skills, and methods to eliminate reversals.

NATHHAN News
(NATional cHallenged Homeschoolers Associated Network)
NATHHAN, 5383 Alpine Road SE, Olalla, WA 98359
Cost: $25 donation for membership including a quarterly magazine.
   A Christian non-profit organization dedicated to providing encouragement to families with special needs children who are homeschooling.

TEACHING FROM A BIBLICAL WORLDVIEW PERSPECTIVE

Everyone has a way of viewing the world around them. This is called your worldview. All of your experiences to this point have shaped and molded the way you think and act. A person develops either a secular worldview (devoid of the truth of the Bible) or a Biblical (Christian) worldview. Although I was not homeschooled, my parents made sure we were raised from a Biblical worldview perspective. All of our discussions about the problems and issues of our lives were related to Biblical standards. As I was growing up I wasn't always thrilled with that since many times it meant not participating in events which "everyone else" was allowed to participate. But now, more than ever, I appreciate the role models they were, and continue to be, as we strive to meet the same standard in our family. If teaching a Biblical worldview to your children is important to you then the following resources should be helpful.

A word of caution: Often Christians cloister themselves within the family and church and don't properly prepare their children for what they will be exposed to in the world, especially if college is in the picture. Be aware of what is out there. At the right time, usually high school, seriously expose the beliefs of the world in the light of the Biblical truths. All of these books should be on your must read list.

Understanding The Times, by David Noebel
General availability
Cost: $36.99 Hardbound 912 pages
Grades: High School

continued on following page

Worldview is any ideology, philosophy, theology, movement, or religion that provides an overarching approach to understanding God, the world, and man's relations to God and the world.
— David Noebel, *Understanding the Times*

Parallels the belief system of the Biblical Christian, Marxist/
Leninist, New Age, and the secular humanist worldviews in
the areas of theology, philosophy, ethics, biology, psychology,
sociology, law, politics, and history.

*Let Us Highly Resolve... The Call to Courage and Determination as
We Prepare to Enter Into the 21st Century*, by David and Shirley Quine
General availability and Cornerstone Curriculum Project
Cost: $10.00
Grades: Parent Resource
A foundational book for preparing families to enter the 21st
century.

*How Should We Then Live? The Rise and Decline of Western Thought
and Culture*, by Francis Schaeffer
General availability
Cost: $14.99
Grades: High School and adult
A philosophical analysis of earlier eras; how the people's
worldviews affected thought and artforms, how they still
affect us today, and how Christians should respond.

Genesis: Finding Our Roots, by Ruth Beechick
Available through Education Services
Cost: $17.50 / hardcover
Grades: Parent Resource
This consists of six unit studies on Genesis 1 - 11 which inte-
grate Bible with history and other subjects. Provides the an-
swers from Genesis to the complicated worldview questions.

Worldview Academy Leadership Camp
P.O. Box 5032, Bryan, TX 77805 / (800) 241-1123
Cost: $345.00 for 1 week
Ages: 13 and up
Equips students in worldview, apologetics/evangelism and ser-
vant leadership. Students learn in the classroom and then
experience "iron sharpening iron," applying what they've
learned in various practicums.

The task of
Christian
leadership is to
confront modern
man with the
Christian
world-life view.
— Carl F. H. Henry

Summit Ministries
P.O. Box 207, Manitou Springs, CO 80829
(719) 685-9103
> The originator of the concept of worldview educational camps. Trains high school students to carefully compare the prevailing worldviews so they are competent to defend their Christian worldview in college and beyond. Uses *Understanding The Times* as their text (written by the founder of the ministry, David Noebel.)

USING LEARNING CENTERS AS A RESOURCE

From the time we began homeschooling, we began creating little corners of opportunity in our home (learning centers). These are special places that contain just the right equipment for exploring and expanding their knowledge in whatever area the children choose. Some of these include an area for science equipment, one for games, another for writing and computer work, and also a general art center.

We allow and encourage the children to use these areas as often as they like. These times spark imagination creativity, and critical thinking, in ways nothing else can. In general they are very careful with the equipment. There are times, however, when we've had to replace things. But, we believe that none of these items would be worth anything if we didn't let them be used.

A very important observation worth mentioning is this - during the times when we concentrated more heavily on books, these centers were deserted. By the time they finished "school" they wanted a wide separation from anything resembling learning. We'd find cobwebs and dust bunnies taking over. Once we were truly converted to our learning lifestyle, these areas became alive again with creativity. The biggest problem is getting the dining room table cleared of their projects in time for supper.

RECOMMENDED RESOURCE

How to Set Up Learning Centers in Your Home, by Mary Hood
General availability or Elijah Company
Cost: $5.00

CHAPTER SIX

ADVICE TO PARENTS OF PRESCHOOLERS

Recently, a mother told me that before she began home educating, a woman exclaimed to her how wonderful her homeschool days would be. She painted a cozy picture of baby on mommy's lap, toddler quietly playing at her feet, while she thoroughly instructs Jr. about the concepts behind long division. After beginning homeschooling, she found her experience to be nothing like that cozy picture. More often than not, those moments turned into baby squirming around, reaching, grabbing, pulling, and tearing the math books and toddler throwing toys, picking at Jr.'s pant legs, and untying Jr.'s shoe laces. Of course, the result was a frenzied, very frustrated mom shouting, "Calgon, take me away!!"

Of course, the woman painted a very idealistic picture and unless you have very compliant children, you know it's not reality. Consequently, one of the most common questions I hear is "How can I teach my children with my preschooler, toddler, and baby around?" I always detect a note of frustration and exasperation in the mother's voice. While it is a fact that teaching with younger siblings around is a difficult challenge at best and some days down right discouraging, it is also (or should be) a very rich experience. So much hinges on attitude and organizational planning in order to make the rich experiences more frequent than the discouragements.

ATTITUDE

Many moms seem to act as if preschool siblings are simply the "cross" they must bear during their homeschool experience.

Other mothers have been known to use them as their "excuse" for ending their home education program altogether. In both cases the moms are already beginning to harbor resentment toward their younger children rather than seeing them as educational tools and positive contributors to their homeschool.

ADVANTAGES TO HAVING PRESCHOOLERS IN THE HOME

1. Younger siblings make an instant audience for the older children.
2. Younger siblings can be scientific guinea pigs for "safe" experiments and projects. They love to be involved!
3. Younger siblings make enthusiastic "listeners" while the older children practice their oral reading.
4. The more children there are in a family the better your dramatizing experiences will be.
5. Older children grow up knowing and bonding better with their younger siblings. They will begin building life-long relationships and learn how to honor those who are younger and weaker.
6. Older children "get" to practice being a proper role model for younger siblings. They begin to see the consequences of improper modeling. For example: After picking on his little sister for a sufficient amount of time, he experiences her picking on him in the same manner. Hopefully, he will conclude that if he sets a better example, her behavior will change. (Great in theory. This one takes several years to cultivate.)
7. Conflicts between older and younger siblings provide the catalyst necessary to force family members to analyze "why" they are having difficulties getting along and hopefully come up with some constructive solutions.
8. Children can learn positive socialization in a controlled environment rather than negative socialization by peers (see Chapter Nine, "What About Socialization?"). In most cases it will take plenty of consistent guidance and discipline from the parents to make this a positive experience. Your family unit will be a "prep school" for learning how to deal with society

outside of the home (see Chapter Nine, "Exposure to the Real World").

9. Younger siblings can force us to mature in patience, flexibility, and control.
10. The entire family will learn to be tolerant of another person's unique personality unless the need for discipline is required.
11. As the family diligently prays and works together with a goal of growing in respect and love for each other, wonder of wonders, it "eventually" works!

Realistically, a positive attitude will not always be possible to maintain. Certain days just seem to be disasters! When everyone is fighting, crying, whining, and yelling, it's easy to throw up your hands in despair and give up. If your number of "disaster days" are becoming all too frequent, maybe you need to devise a plan to get it under control.

ORGANIZATIONAL PLANNING

Many mothers diligently plan lessons for their school-age children. They feel pretty confident about how they've organized each child's schedule to complete the lessons and activities that are planned for each day. They feel good about the time they've spent planning and organizing, trusting this will make for a smooth day. Then along comes little brother or sister and the papers get torn (or colored on), the manipulatives fall to the floor, the yelling and screaming starts, and the tears begin to flow from both mom and the kids. After all that careful planning, what went wrong? The answer is quite simple. You planned for your older children but not for your younger children. Just because they are not compulsory school age doesn't mean you won't have to plan for them. As a matter of fact, it's possible to spend more time planning for them than for your older and more independent children. Don't become discouraged by this realization. After the initial organizing phase, it becomes easier and more natural. The extra amount of planning will eventually pay off in the form of a smoother operating, and less frustrating, homeschool day.

In planning for your preschool children (including toddlers and babies), you need to have a clear focus regarding what you want to accomplish. Although your goal is to keep your child "occupied" so you can effectively instruct your older children with a minimum of interruptions, guard against the attitude of just "getting rid" of them. Plan activities that will make that time worthwhile and productive for the youngster.

PRESCHOOLERS: AGES FOUR AND FIVE

Preschool children about four and five years of age (some three-year-olds, too) will greatly benefit from activities that will set a foundation for future learning of reading, writing, and arithmetic skills. When your child is school age, you will find that he will be easier to teach because of the competency he has attained through pre-reading, pre-writing, and pre-arithmetic awareness.

Unfortunately, many parents have the mistaken idea that when their children reach the "magic" age of five or six, they will be able to easily adapt to reading, writing, and arithmetic workbook assignments. When this doesn't happen, it can be very frustrating. Usually the problem stems from little or no foundational skill building. A child needs ample time to experientially develop:

- visual discrimination: ability to "see" differences and similarities; a skill necessary to distinguish between a "b" and a "d" while reading and writing.
- auditory discrimination: ability to "hear" differences and similarities; a skill necessary to distinguish between the short "e" sound and the short "i" sound in reading and language usage.
- eye-hand coordination: ability to synchronize what the eye is seeing and what the hand is doing; a skill necessary to achieve good handwriting techniques.
- left-to-right sequencing: practice in moving the eyes from left to right; a skill necessary for reading.
- small muscle control: a skill necessary for writing.
- making predictions: a skill necessary for reading comprehension and math problem solving.

There are parents that try to teach concepts or skills too early and consequently frustrate the child.

— June Oberlander
Slow and Steady, Get Me Ready

- one-to-one correspondence: ability to match items one-to-one; a skill necessary to mentally organize and count for use in mathematics.

When these skills, and many others are developed, the transition into more formalized reading, writing, and arithmetic is made easier and more natural.

These skills cannot be successfully mastered by using a lot of workbooks. Children, especially young children, learn best by doing and discovering through play (the child's workshop). The child's immediate environment is full of fascinating objects with which to experiment and to explore. With some preparation and guidance on your part, your child's everyday experiences can be turned into useful learning games. As a nice side benefit, your child's absorption in these games will free you up to attend to the needs of your older children without the guilt of feeling you are neglecting your younger one. At the end of this chapter you will find a list of books that explain how to guide your child's learning experiences and actually make these games from simple things that are around your home.

Some parents complain that they don't have time to prepare these homemade items. Believe me, you don't have time not to prepare! Your investment of time in this will save you many frustrating moments later on when you are trying to teach an intensive concept to your older child while your preschooler is pulling at your skirt. One suggestion to alleviate the time-crunch is to allow your older children and preschoolers to help make these items. Your older children will be reinforcing their own skills while motivating and encouraging your younger children just by showing an interest in their games. Allowing your younger child to be involved in this will cultivate a greater appreciation for his "school work" and will convey the message that what he does has importance.

Another way to make your preschooler feel important, rather than a burden, is to take time to work with him first. Take 15 - 30 minutes to get him set up with his learning games. This can be done while your older child is completing chores or working independently. One mother recently told me that doing this relieved her of the guilt feelings she used to have about neglecting her younger child. Now when her preschooler begins wanting extra attention at an inappropriate time, she simply reminds her that she spent time with her first and now it's her sister's turn. This doesn't always satisfy her younger child, but she feels confident that she is now dividing her attention appropriately and, if necessary, she can confidently discipline her child.

Whenever possible, do include your younger children in the activities in which the older children are involved. Teaching via the unit studies method is especially conducive to this (see Chapter Two: "The Unit Study Method"). Reserve the learning games for times when you will be focusing your attention on your older children. This will also keep you from interfering and pressuring your preschooler to hurry up or perform faster. After all, the purpose of these games is to let your child learn to discover, think, and come to conclusions independently. Remember, however, that your preschooler will need to discuss his findings with you and ask you questions related to his activities. These discussions are important for building his language and vocabulary skills. So take frequent breaks from your older child to listen and respond to your preschooler. Encourage him to share his discoveries with the entire family and be sure to praise, praise, praise!

Toddlers: Ages Two and Three

Definitely, toddlers are a trickier age. The toddler has a shorter attention span and a lower tolerance for allowing you to give your attention elsewhere. You will find it necessary to have many activities ready so he can easily move from one to another as his interests change. These activities can include some of those you already have prepared for your four- or five-year old. The books recommended for making these games do have activities suitable for the two- and three-year old. Elaborate activities are not necessary for this age. You'll find that water play and sand play using measuring cups, sieves, and squirt bottles will build a child's observing and exploring skills while keeping him very happy and content. Pegboards and LEGO® building blocks will build visual discrimination skills. Listening to tapes and speaking into a tape recorder will build auditory discrimination.

Zipping, buttoning, coloring, painting, cutting and pasting will build fine motor skills. (*KONOS Compass* has more suggestions like these. See Appendix B.)

At this age the greatest amount of disciplinary action may be needed. Two- and three-year olds are naturally going to test their boundaries. Your child may find this a great opportunity and take great delight in seeing what he can get away with while Mommy is busy with big sister. This may emerge in the form of sneaking away and getting into "off limit" items or just simply pestering until he has everyone's full attention (and aggravation, I might add). You will need to set firm boundaries and limits on this type of behavior. Never threaten! Always follow through with what you have established as consequences for unacceptable behavior. By all means, be the authority or you will lose control and find your homeschool experience to be extremely frustrating. When you demand and expect cooperation and respect, you are much more likely to receive it. For further study, refer to the books recommended on discipline at the end of this section.

BABIES: INFANTS AND THE ONE YEAR OLD

Ahhh, the one-year old! Truly, this age offers another challenge and another opportunity to grow in patience, flexibility, and control. Babies are inquisitive and want to be involved. That is just their nature and they shouldn't be any other way. We, as parents, must find creative ways to channel that inquisitiveness so they are not allowed to infringe upon others' rights.

If your baby is a sleeper, you have it made! It's relatively easy to plan your times of intensive instruction around your baby's nap schedule. Fortunately, all of our babies took two-hour morning naps. That is when I would teach the older children. During their independent study time, I would be free to play learning games with our preschooler and toddler.

But babies grow out of their morning nap and a new phase begins. Baby will become more and more a part of the morning routine. Preschoolers, if you have any, can be very helpful with occupying the baby with toys, and some of her learning games. As they play you will notice that the older sibling explains and demonstrates objects and activities. She is role playing the part of a teacher. Baby loves the attention and "teacher" builds her vocabulary and communication skills. If you have more children, you may want to give each child a designated time to spend with the baby. If you portray this time as a privilege rather than a duty, all the children will have a positive experience and you will be free to work on an individual basis with each child.

If your baby is not a sleeper, don't despair. There are still ways to cope and have a productive homeschool day. You would be wise to teach your baby early to be comfortable in a play pen or play yard. This can be very helpful during the morning instructional period. Other families have found doorway gates to be helpful. This keeps the baby confined to a room, attached to the school area, where he is free to explore, and he is still within your sights for safety measures. This should help eliminate refereeing the wrestling matches for pens, pencils, papers, and manipulatives. Make sure you don't ignore your baby or any of your preschoolers for that matter. Most of the negative behavior takes place because they feel neglected and slighted. Take plenty of breaks from the older child and spend some time playing with, cuddling, and directing your youngster's activities. Just a few minutes at a time is all it takes. Most of the time this will satisfy their need for mommy's attention. Remember, involve them in the school activities just as much as you can.

Extra Tips

1. Younger children love to play "school." We keep educational toys in a special cabinet in our school area. They include toys such as pegboard and pegs, blocks, shape sorters, magnetic letters and numbers, wooden letter and number puzzles, plastic animals, nesting cups and more. Rotating new toys into the cabinet from time to time helps prevent boredom. If you are short on storage space you can purchase an inexpensive, under-the-bed storage box (or cut one down to size) and store the toys in a bedroom.

2. I'll pass along an important piece of advice my mother gave me years ago when our first child was going through a fussy stage. It has been something I have clung to when I have felt hopelessly discouraged. "Honey," she said, "it's only a phase. Soon he'll be out of that and on to something new." It sounds simplistic but it is so profound. So, don't despair, the problems you may be dealing with now will eventually pass on into a new phase. There is hope in knowing that the problems won't last forever. This releases you to concentrate on the good times you are having.

3. Provide for positive and loving experiences so you and the children can enjoy this precious time together. You are building relationships. What you do now will affect those relationships for a lifetime.

WHEN ALL ELSE FAILS

You've readjusted your attitude and you have your plans all mapped out. Okay, so what happens on those days when all your positive attitudes and all your great plans just don't work and you just aren't up to dealing with it? (Be prepared, you'll have those days occasionally.) My advice is to stop what you're doing and change your course. Go to the park, go for a car or bike ride, visit some friends or relatives, play a game, or watch a video. *One hint:* Be in control of your emotions enough to let the children think it is all your idea. Don't let on that it's because of their behavior. They'll catch on very quickly and start making a habit out of playing the "let's get Mom so frustrated that she'll take us to the park" game. Kids are so savvy, aren't they?

It is important to realize that everyone needs a break from the routine now and then to just unwind and regroup. Relax and enjoy your day out and have confidence in the fact that tomorrow is a new day and a chance for a fresh start.

If mothers could learn to do for themselves what they do for their children... Let the mother go out to play! ...have courage to let everything go when life becomes too tense, and just take a day, or half a day, out in the fields, or with a favorite book... life would go on far more happily for both children and parents.

— Charlotte Mason

BOOKS ON HOW TO MAKE LEARNING GAMES

The following are some resources to use with your preschooler. Check your library for many of these books. I have included the card catalog numbers for your convenience. You may find many available through general homeschool mail-order catalogs. See Appendix B for the contact information.

Child's Play: An Activities and Materials Handbook,
by Barbara Trencher   J372.13 TR

Games for Reading: Playful Ways to Help Your Child Read,
by Peggy Kaye ($14.00) 649.58 KA or General availability.

Home Grown Kids, by Dr. Raymond and Dorothy Moore
Library or General availability
Cost: $9.00
> Learning activities are suggested in Part Two, chapters 3-9.

Learning Activities for Preschool Children: A Home Teaching Handbook for Parents and Teachers, by Ellen B. DeFranco
> Excellent book if you can find it. It was out of print last time I checked. Published originally by Olympus Publishing Company in Salt Lake City, Utah (801-583-3666.)

Learning Games for Infants and Toddlers, by Dr. J Ronald Lally and Dr. Ira J. Gordon   649.68 LA

Living and Learning With Children, by Paula Jorde 372.21 JO

Playtime Learning Games for Young Children, by Alice Honig 649.58 HO

Slow and Steady, Get Me Ready, by June Oberlander
General availability
Cost: $17.95
> Weekly activities from birth through four years of age.

Teaching Montessori in the Home: The Preschool Years and
The Elementary Years (two separate books), by Hainstock
371.3078HA

Workjobs, by Mary Baratta-Lorton
Library or Addison-Wesley
Cost: $19.95
    Workjobs is my absolute favorite. I've used it the most.

PARENT RESOURCES

A Home Start In Reading, An Easy Start In Arithmetic, and *A Strong Start In Language*, by Ruth Beechick.
General availability and Education Services
Cost: $4.00 each or $12.00 for the set
    Helpful ideas to satisfy your eager young learner.

The New Dare to Discipline, by Dr. James Dobson
Library, Christian Book Store, or general availability.
Cost: $12.99

Home Built Discipline, Home Grown Kids, and *Home Style Teaching*,
by Dr. Raymond and Dorothy Moore.
Libraries, Christian bookstores, or General availability.

The Piaget Handbook for Teachers and Parents: Children in the Age of Discovery, by Rosemary Peterson and Victoria Felton-Collins
372.241 PE

The Strong-Willed Child, by Dr. James Dobson.
Available in libraries or Christian book stores.
Cost: $11.99

Teaching Preschoolers (ages 2-3) and *Teaching Kindergartners*
(ages 4-5), by Dr. Ruth Beechick
General availability and Education Services
Cost: $9.00 each

MAGAZINES AND NEWSPAPERS
JUST FOR YOUR PRESCHOOLER

Your Big Backyard
National Wildlife Foundation
P.O. Box 777, Mount Morris, IL 61054   (800) 588-1650
Cost: Monthly for about $10.00 per year
   A preschool science magazine.

Weekly Reader (Pre-K edition)
3001 Cindel Drive, Delran, NJ 08370 / (800) 446-3355
Cost: 28 issues per year for $24.95
   Interactive activities to build foundational skills. Does not
   require reading or writing on the part of the child. Older children can easily use this to work with the younger siblings.

CHAPTER SEVEN

HOMESCHOOLING YOUR HIGH SCHOOLER

Many parents new to homeschooling have the misconception that once their child reaches ninth grade they must enroll him in a conventional high school or at the very least, an accredited correspondence school. A home education program can start and end whenever you feel it is appropriate for your child. This can mean from preschool all the way through college. However, I would recommend that you check with your state's laws to find out if home educators in your state are bound to keeping credits similar to those kept in the public school system. Make sure the information you receive from the public system agrees with your state homeschool organization's information (see Appendix A). Often the public system, knowingly or not, gives out misinformation regarding this area of homeschooling.

Your next question might very well be, "How in the world will I go about homeschooling my high schooler?" Perhaps your question stems from a fear of not being qualified in all the specialized subjects. Perhaps you fear the record-keeping or that you may not adequately prepare your child for college. You aren't the first to pose these questions. I dreaded the day I would face these issues. Jack and I briefly considered a local private Christian school or a fully prepared and accredited correspondence course. But, we knew that either of those options would take the control of his education away from us and neither choice would be sensitive to our son's gifts, talents, and his own goals and desires. So we chose to continue to homeschool through high school and the rewards have been great! Of course, each family, with their teen's input, must choose the method that will help the individual child meet their own goals for the future.

Wise parents...
help them to
achieve the goals
He implants in
them.
— Jay Kesler,
*Ten Mistakes
Parents Make
With Teenagers*

I guess since forever, it has been natural for parents to try and steer their young adults towards what they think is best for them. Haven't we been doing that all along? Aren't we just thinking of their best interests? Probably the hardest part about homeschooling a high schooler is all the unknowns concerning the future. We try to get our children to set goals at the tender age of 13 so we can make sure they take all the right courses so they can apply to all the right colleges. We want to prepare them for all the options...just in case! But, how many 13-year olds are mature enough, or wise enough to know what direction they will want to take five years into the future? Do we even want to burden them with those decisions?

I have to admit that, not considering this when our son reached 9th grade, I sat down with pen and pad in hand and said, "O.K. It's time to get serious! Let's set some goals. First, what do you want to be when you grow up? My son's expression was a look some-where between wonder and panic. His response, "How should I know?" as if to say, "Do I have to decide that today?" and "What if I change my mind? Will that mess up everything? Will I have to start all over?" That was a loaded question, wasn't it? Don't get me wrong, setting goals is very important, but easing into the dis-cussion with a light conversation and no flip charts and diagrams would be a little less intimidating.

Now it was my turn to panic! How could I plan his high school program if I didn't know what he was heading for? O.K. then, I thought, I will just have to prepare him for every possible option. Let's see, that means if he wants to be a plumber, I'll have to arrange for an apprenticeship. If he wants to be in the medical profession I'll have to make sure he spends some time volunteering at a local hospital. Maybe a musician or artist... I'll put him in lessons. What about a pastor or missionary? I'll send him off on one of those short-term, summer mission trips. Oh, what if he wants to be an engineer? I'll have to make sure he has lots of higher math. Maybe he'll want to discover a cure for can-cer. I'll have to make sure he takes plenty of the sciences, espe-cially chemistry. I know...what about a rocket scientist... can't forget the physics! Whew! That train of thought would scare any mom away from the thought of homeschooling her high schooler.

> Don't consider your kid some *thing* that's going to fulfill some aspiration of yours.
> — Jay Kesler
> *Ten Mistakes Parents Make With Teenagers*

> Most of the expectations we have of our teenagers are things we've spent our whole lives learning.
> — Jay Kesler,
> *Ten Mistakes Parents Make With Teenagers*

Let's be realistic! We cannot, and I believe should not, try to prepare our teens for every option. Not only would it be frustrating for you, but it would be even more so for your child. So, how do you go about planning then? First, consider your teen's favorite hobbies, play activities, likes, and dislikes. Does your teen spend a lot of time at the computer or out of doors? Does your teen prefer to work alone or with other people? Does your teen prefer to lead or to follow?

The answers to these questions may help you and your teen together, to at least, rule out many career choices. For example, our son is the outdoorsy type and knows he doesn't want a desk job where he would have to show up with a suit and tie each day. He knows he wants a job that would take him outdoors at least part of the day. He is very service oriented and loves to be with people; definitely not a loner. Strong leadership skills have been developed, but at this point he doesn't think he wants to be an entrepreneur, although he hasn't ruled out the possibility for the future. He would like a job where his leadership skills would allow him to "climb the ladder" so to speak. Although Tim has taken upper level math courses, he doesn't have a real bent or desire to pursue that area. That would rule out the rocket scientist for sure!

Thinking these things through will allow you and your teen to narrow the possibilities and consider appropriate curriculum choices, apprenticeships, or part-time jobs. Our son Tim, has joined our city's Fire/Rescue Explorer program. This is a mentorship/apprenticeship program in which he'll be trained in CPR and fire service and then allowed to participate with the firefighters and paramedics on their calls. The biology and chemistry courses he took are good foundations for his future paramedic training. He already speaks with anticipation about becoming a Battalion Chief someday. (There are those leadership qualities shining through.) Participation in this will either verify or nullify his desires to become a firefighter/paramedic. If he decides it's not for him, it is better to find out now. If he decides it is what he wants to do, then the experience will be an advantage toward being hired.

It doesn't disappoint us in the least that he's not planning on attending an Ivy League college to become a famous rocket scientist. Most kids won't! We're very proud of him and his aspirations to serve his fellow man in a career which will challenge him and make him happy.

Don't be surprised if the narrowing-down-the-field process takes a year or two. Most teens are dealing too intensely with hormones, mood swings, and pimples to be worried too much about a career. If your teen is in this situation just allow him to work on the typical required courses to fulfill credits toward a diploma or a college transcript. (The next section will deal with credits and graduation options.) After your teen has a stronger notion of where his interests might lead him, begin to set some serious goals and time frames. Figure into those goals his preparation for the PSAT and SAT and/or ACT (college entrance exams) if college figures into the picture. At this point your teen should begin to concentrate heavily on home courses, tutored courses, or correspondence courses and/or to begin an appropriate apprenticeship. Most kids are about 15 or 16 years old at this point. Dedication, perseverance, and initiative are appropriate character traits for the teen to develop at this stage if they are not already established.

Next, decide on a record-keeping system that will work for you both (see the end of this chapter). Train your student to handle as much of the record-keeping as possible. Keep some sort of a portfolio or notebook to house a list of books which have been read, titles of curriculum, and samples of the students work along with any special achievements or accomplishments, community service acknowledgments, 4-H participation, apprenticeships, etc. This portfolio can double as a ready-made college or job resume.

HIGH SCHOOL GRADUATION OPTIONS

Probably the most common high school question I hear asked is in regard to graduation requirements. Most states require between 19 and 24 credits to graduate from their *public* schools. Your library provides your state statutes to find the exact number for each subject.

Typical requirements look something like this:

English	3 - 4	Mathematics	2 - 3
Science (with Lab)	2 - 3	Practical Arts	1
American History	1	World History	1
U.S. Government	½	Economics	½
Physical Education	½	Performing Arts	1
Life Management Skills	½	Electives	6 - 9

A credit is defined as a minimum of 150 hours (180 in many states) of instruction in a course of study. How that instruction is given in the homeschool setting varies widely. Most states won't award diplomas to homeschoolers even if you follow their rigid hours and credit systems. We don't feel any obligation to do so. Even in an unschooling environment, you will find that you will be able to fulfill all the subjects by merely integrating learning with your living. We emphasize content vs. hours.

The goal is to produce your own diploma awarded from your homeschool. You will also need to produce a portfolio and a transcript that would be acceptable for college entrance, if indeed college is the goal. It is clearly evident, by many examples around the country, that home-produced diplomas and transcripts are very acceptable at most colleges. This trend began with Grant Colfax in the early 80's. Read his family's story in *Homeschooling For Excellence*, by David and Micki Colfax, ($10.99). I know one homeschooled young man in our city who received a four-year athletic and academic scholarship to Florida Atlantic University (a state school) beginning in the Fall 1996. Another received a full four-year academic scholarship at the University of Miami (a private school) for Fall 1996. It is interesting to note that the young man attending U of M was accepted at several other prestigious schools around the nation. Georgia Tech called to ask if they could use his home-made transcript as a sample for other homeschool applicants to follow. We've come a long way!

In creating a transcript with grades and credits you need to establish an explainable standard. Here is where you can get creative. Nothing says you have to follow the public school standard as cited above. For those of you following a less conventional approach to schooling (see below), you will want to create your own standard, but it should still be explainable. To give you direction in this area you should read, *Senior High: A Home-Designed Form+U+la* or *Home School, High School, and Beyond* (see end of chapter). There is freedom in their "structured" record-keeping system which allows for your not-so-traditional method of learning.

Keep in mind you do have options regarding the manner in which you instruct your high schooler. The following are typical variations:

Conventional — This usually means following an accredited high school correspondence course with a textbook for each subject. You may enroll your child in a program such as American School, University of Nebraska, or North Dakota State University (see Appendix B for contact information). Your child will receive a diploma upon the successful completion of his program. For some teens this method may be necessary based on their choices regarding their future educational or career plans. It is important to find out early on (if possible) whether a diploma from an accredited high school will be mandatory. For example, a family in this area has a daughter who was a swimmer and was trying out for the Olympics during her homeschooling high school years. NCAA rules would not accept a GED so she took a correspondence course from University of Nebraska. Also, the armed forces prefer a diploma from a high school but will accept the GED under certain conditions. Check with your local recruiting office because a change is being considered.

Some families using the conventional approach simply purchase the necessary texts and write their own transcripts.

Private School Umbrella — This in an agreement between a homeschool and a private school whereby reports are submitted and a transcript and/or diploma is awarded when the agreement is satisfied. Check with your state laws to see if this is a permissible option especially if you plan to go under an umbrella school whose headquarters are outside of your state.

Dual Enrollment For College Credit — Dual enrollment is when a high school student is simultaneously enrolled in college courses in either a community college, state university, or private college. The credits earned are counted toward both the high school diploma and a college degree. Some states, such as Florida, give all qualified high school students, including homeschoolers, free tuition. Check to see if this is an option in your state. This can give your child the opportunity to accelerate his education by completing at least a portion of his college credits while still in high school. And, as in the case of Florida, it would be tuition-free. This might be a way to allow your teen to take upper level courses that you do not feel qualified to teach and at the same time ease him into college life. Students most likely will be required to take placement tests to see if they qualify and can handle college level courses.

GED Test — This is not an instructional option but I mention it here because passing this test is equivalent to receiving a high school diploma. This would circumvent having to meet any required number of credits necessary to graduate from the conventional school system. Make sure your child's future plans will allow a GED. Although there still seems to be a negative stigma attached to this, it is fading as more quality homeschoolers opt for this diploma, eliminating the mentality that GED equals dropout. This diploma is based on academic skill and not attendance in a classroom. It proves your child actually knows something and hasn't just been warming a seat for thirteen years.

Call your local adult and community education centers to obtain information about test centers, registration, and GED preparatory classes. Also inquire about the minimum age for taking the test. In Florida the stated age is 18, but exceptions are made for home educators to take it at 16 years of age, since this is the age compulsory attendance ends.

A practice test is usually taken to identify weak areas and then remedial classes are offered. The classes are not mandatory and could easily be implemented in your home as part of your home education program. Practice books are easily obtained from libraries or general homeschool mail-order catalog companies. One such guide is *The Complete GED Preparation Book* ($18.95). Available through general homeschool mail-order catalogs.

One thing to keep in mind about the GED is that it is a source for college scholarship money. Even if you intend to keep credits and/or work through an accredited correspondence course you can still take the GED and try for the scholarship that is awarded to those with high scores.

The national office for the GED test is:

American Council in Education
One Dupont Circle NW, Suite 250, Washington, DC 20036
(202) 939-9490

Learning Lifestyle or Unschooling — This instructional style allows the student to explore his own talents and interests rather than trying to cover every conventional subject. This could include apprenticeships. If college bound, an extensive portfolio may be useful to prove effort and mastery rather than a rigid counting of hours. As mentioned earlier, many colleges are now accepting home-produced transcripts without question or concern. Homeschool, by nature, is a learning environment and would more than meet the minimum hours. The Colfaxes did it this way! Read their story in their book, *Homeschooling for Excellence* ($10.99).

Alternatives to Conventional Schooling — Many parents of high school students have mentioned that it is their observation that a good portion of high school (especially eleventh and twelfth grades) seems to be a big repeat, and therefore, a waste of their child's time. As a former high school teacher, I tend to agree with that observation to a certain extent. Neither the parents to whom I have spoken nor I believe a young person should drop out of school and just flounder on their own. A practical alternative to "more years of the same" is to get the child involved in an intensive enrichment program related to career orientation. I'm not just talking about a vocational technical school, although that may be part of the plan. A program similar to what I am referring is sponsored by Bill Gothard's Advanced Training Institute International (ATII) (see Appendix B), but can easily be accomplished on your own.

If a child has been properly educated (not just socially promoted) and has average grades, that child should have covered academic basics by about the tenth or eleventh grade. This is especially true with homeschoolers because of the tendency to accelerate the education process via the tutorial situation. Also, the homeschooling family typically has the assurance of knowing they have taught their teen *how to learn*. They can feel confident that throughout his lifetime he will be able to easily pursue any course of study of interest to him, thus constantly expanding his knowledge. The latter years of high school are typically the time in the teen's life when he is excited about getting out and trying his hand at a few things. Yet, we discourage that by saying, "No, you have to sit in a classroom (or homeschool) for two more years." It's no wonder kids are so discouraged and so many are dropping out. I certainly remember feeling that way and looking at the prospect of two more years. At that age, two years seems like a lifetime! These kids are smart enough to know that most of what is being taught is just repeated material at a slightly higher level. If we have diligently taught our children "how" to learn, we can encourage them to continue learning while pursuing their interests and future career choices.

So, what is the alternative? Why not involve these young people in a high school program that includes and encourages apprenticeships, short-term missions, interscholastic extracurricular activities, cottage industries, and possibly dual-enrollment in college? We are one among many families doing all or part of these in a very successful manner and the children are truly flourishing. Of course, all of this is executed under the steady guidance of the parents, ever watchful of how the teen is affected.

College Involvement: This is usually done in the junior and senior year. College credits can also be applied to their high school credits (See "Dual Enrollment" mentioned above). This allows exposure to what college would be like as he decides what he wants to do with his future. These credits are transferable when the teen continues with his college education.

Missions Involvement: Short-term missions is a very exciting and enriching opportunity for your teen. While working for the Lord he will experience other lands and other cultures. What an education! It may even spark a commitment to go into full-time

If you want (your children) to spend some time getting well-rounded and enlarging their frame of reference, send them on a short-term missions project to another culture.
— Michael Farris, *The Homeschooling Father*

mission work. If you are interested in this option, call organizations such as Youth With A Mission (503) 364-3837, or Teen Mania Ministries (800) 329-FIRE. Our son highly recommends Teen Mania. He has participated in their mission program and his spiritual life, sense of priorities, and leadership abilities have been very positively affected.

Apprenticeship Involvement: An apprentice is simply someone who is learning by practical experience under skilled workers. Wouldn't it be wonderful if our teens could experience various forms of work before deciding on a lifetime career? It only makes sense. How many times do we hear of people who spend years in college and then find out they don't even like the profession they chose. An apprenticeship program exposes the young person to careers like carpentry, plumbing, secretarial work, hair dressing, computer technology, child care, veterinary work, medicine, dentistry, law, and a whole array of other occupations. Of course, you will have to find people willing to let your teen "tag along", maybe even as a volunteer, but many are happy to work with you on at least a short-term basis. All of this will probably lead to a decision to attend a college, a vocational technical school, or maybe even start a business. For complete information on this option consider *Apprenticeship Plus*, by Inge Cannon, $65.00 (see Appendix B). It is a nine-hour audio seminar with a 135-page notebook. It includes more than just apprenticeship information such as preparing a resume and creating transcripts.

Interscholastic Extracurricular Student Activities: Check with your state organization to find out whether this option is open to you. This enables homeschoolers to participate in public and private school activities such as sports, band, cheerleading, drama, speech, foreign language clubs, etc. Your teen may be able to join as an individual or as a homeschool team.

Cottage Industries: This is basically a business run from the home. It could be anything from a dog-walking service to writing computer programs. Apprenticing could very well motivate a young person to pursue a small business. This real-life educational experience can teach more than any textbook could ever

> Apprenticeship offers far superior advantages to collegiate instruction in one very important area — the training and development of godly character.
> — Michael Farris, *The Homeschooling Father*

expound upon regarding money management, business relationships, organizational skills, and more. Amazingly enough (or maybe not so amazingly), many young people have turned their small businesses into full-time, well-paying adult careers. You might consider giving this book as a gift to your young entrepreneur: *Business by the Book - The Complete Guide of Biblical Principles for Business Men and Women,* by Larry Burkett ($15.95). Available in some mail-order catalogs or at your local Christian book store.

Perhaps this whole concept of non-conventional schooling deviates from what you imagined the typical homeschool high school program should be. Maybe it even sounds a bit overwhelming. We are convinced that the benefits it reaps make it well worth the effort. However, if you allow your teen to pursue his interests you will find effort is replaced with self-motivation and an enjoyable learning environment. We are continually encouraged by the success stories we hear from families implementing this course of study, including the successes our son is experiencing (see Chapter Three for Tim's story). If the proof is in the proverbial pudding, we are happy with the recipe.

While it is not for everyone, this enrichment program could certainly be pursued by either the traditional student or the GED graduate. Unfortunately, the traditional student may find it difficult to take time away from his heavy schedule of book work.

Combination — Combining two or more of the above methods is probably the most common means of meeting graduation requirements. Transcripts can be designed by the homeschool. See book titles listed below for help with transcripts.

Note: Whatever method you use for high school graduation, remember that when college is in the future, it is important to prepare accordingly. Check the admissions requirements at the college of your choice. It will usually require some upper level math and some foreign language. Don't forget to consider seriously your teen's input and then base your decisions on his possible career choices for the future. After all, *his* future happiness is what you are after. Since most colleges require SAT or ACT scores, ensure readiness by working through the available practice tests mentioned below.

College Bound

Many parents fear their children will not be able to attend college if they have educated them at home during the high school years. Parents worry that if they can't show a "real" diploma then college is out of the question. As mentioned above, diplomas and transcripts for homeschooled teens are obtainable and/or you can create your own, so do not allow this to be a concern. In reality, colleges base their acceptance of students primarily on college entrance exam scores and a transcript (although a diploma is sometimes required). If your teen has any trouble at all entering a college with a GED, you can circumvent this by attendance in a community college for one semester and then entering as a transfer student. The best way to plan is to call the college your teen is considering and find out what they require and work from that point.

An encouraging note is the fact that colleges are now actively scouting out homeschoolers. Oral Roberts University (ORU) in Tulsa, OK is offering a $6,000 scholarship for home-educated students. You can begin taking correspondence courses while in high school. These courses are fully accredited and transferrable. For information and qualifications call 1-800-678-8876. Another college advertisement offered a $2000 scholarship just for being a homeschooler. Why? Homeschoolers are proving to be desirable on campus because of their leadership abilities, scholastic achievement, moral character, independent study habits, and the list goes on. Kudos!

Scholarships

Speaking of scholarships, there are thousands out there that are available for your student. Many do not require your child to be an "Einstein." Read *Bear's Guide to Finding Money for College*, ($7.95) or check out your local library for many other books on this subject.

Providing a child with a college education merely for the sake of such an education has done little to help young people or our country. The majority of the time and expense of college should be spent for career preparation, not personal enrichment.
— Michael Farris, *The Homeschooling Father*

College Entrance Exams

The two entrance exams most widely used by the colleges are the Admissions Testing Program - ATP (this is the one that includes the Scholastic Aptitude Test - SAT) and the American College Testing (ACT) Assessment Program.

The following information will help you to register your child for the tests:

The **Admissions Testing Program (ATP):** Better known as the **SAT**.

> Contact: **College Board ATP**
> Rosedale Road, Princeton, NJ 08541
> (609) 771-7600

Includes the Scholastic Aptitude Test - SAT (not to be confused with the Stanford Achievement Test given to elementary and secondary students) and fourteen separate achievement tests. The test evaluates not only the student's potential for academic success in college, but also the level of proficiency required of a student leaving high school and entering college. Acceptance scores are determined by the individual colleges. This test is usually taken during the senior year or the year prior to entering college. This test can be taken as many times as needed.

To Register: Go to a local high school and ask the guidance counselor for the registration bulletin and the two free booklets called *Taking the SAT* and *Bulletin for the SAT Program.* They provide sample questions, test dates, testing centers, and individual registration information. Your child does not have to attend that high school or any high school to take these tests.

To Practice: You can purchase practice booklets that contain previously administered tests and strategies for taking the tests. These are available through the general homeschool mail-order catalog companies (see Appendix B). The titles are *Cracking the New SAT and PSAT* at $17.00 and *Real SATs* at $14.00. You may be able to find them in the library. If your teen loves interacting with a computer there are some SAT prep software programs on the market. Our son has one but actually feels he is getting more strategies and better instruction from the *Cracking the New SAT and PSAT* book. He uses the software to get more practice.

SAT PRACTICE SOFTWARE

Your Personal Trainer for SAT
Davidson & Associates (800) 545-7677
Cost: $30.00 - $35.00

Score Builder for SAT
The Learning Company (800) 852-2255
Cost: $45.00 - $55.00

American College Testing (ACT) Assessment Program
          Contact: **ACT Registration**
                        P.O. Box 414, Iowa City, Iowa 52243
                        (319) 337-1270
     This measures overall educational development and performance on work similar to that of a college level. Acceptance scores are determined by the individual colleges. This test is usually taken during the senior year or during the year prior to entering college.

To Register: Ask the local high school guidance counselor for the free information bulletin, individual registration form, and study guide titled *Preparing for the ACT* or contact the ACT Registration at the above address.

To Practice: Purchase the practice book, *Cracking the ACT* at $17.00. Available from general homeschool mail-order catalog companies.

PRACTICE COLLEGE ENTRANCE EXAMS — PSAT

     A practice test companion to the SAT is taken by juniors or during the year before the actual college entrance exams will be administered. The following will help you plan for this test:

Preliminary Scholastic Aptitude Test / National Merit Scholarship Qualification Test

> Contact: **PSAT / NMSQT**
> Rosedale Road, Princeton, NJ 08541
> (609) 771-7070

This is a shortened version of the SAT and measures the scholastic ability of those students considering college. The scores are for the student's own use in planning their education after high school. It also serves as an initial screening for scholarship purposes. Because of this, some parents find it beneficial for their children to first take it in the sophomore year to "get a feel for the test" and make improvements for the one that counts in the junior year. There is no individual registration with the contact agency so you will have to register your child to take the test with the students in a local high school. Your child does not have to attend the high school but be aware that the test scores will be sent to the high school and you will have to make arrangements to pick them up there. Bulletins regarding this test are available in August from the local high school. The test is administered in October.

To Practice: *Cracking the New Sat and PSAT* and *Real SATs* (see above) are both helpful in practicing for the PSAT.

EARNING COLLEGE CREDITS DURING HIGH SCHOOL - AP CLASSES

The **Advanced Placement Program** allows the high school student to pursue college level studies and receive credit when entering college. Individual tests in many different subject areas evaluates sufficient mastery of that subject.

> Contact: **Advanced Placement Program**
> Educational Testing Service
> Rosedale Road, Princeton, NJ 08541
> (609) 734-5292

There is no individual registration so you must register for this test through the local high school. It is given once a year in May. A study guide is available from the contact agency.

As mentioned earlier, another way to earn college credits during high school is through the dual enrollment program (see above).

"CLEP"ING OUT OF COLLEGE COURSES

The CLEP examination (College-Level Examination Program) is given in colleges. It allows a student to prove sufficient mastery of a subject to earn credits without attending the actual class.

Contact: **CLEP Program**
Rosedale Road, Princeton, NJ 08541
(609) 921-9000

Request the names of the colleges that are open test centers from the contact agency listed above. Check with the colleges your child is considering to find out if they honor CLEP scores, which specific CLEP tests are acceptable, and what scores they must achieve. You can purchase the study guide titled, *The Official Study Guide for the CLEP Examination by The College Board*, for $15.00 from your local book store.

COLLEGE AT HOME

For a variety of reasons many parents and students alike prefer getting a college degree at home rather than on a campus. You may not even know this is possible. Many colleges will award a degree based on life experiences and/or based on correspondence work with little or no on-campus attendance. One obvious benefit is the low cost involved. For more information refer to:

Bear's Guide to Non-Traditional College Degrees, by John Bear
General availability
Cost: $25.00

Lists the many colleges that offer correspondence courses for college credit.

The Independent Study Catalog
General availability
Cost: $16.95

> This book catalogs the actual correspondence courses available through colleges.

COLLEGE ALTERNATIVES

Gone are the days when a college degree was the prerequisite to financial success or getting a job. A few months ago our newspaper reported a list of the 20 fastest growing career fields (according to the U.S. Department of Labor). None of those on the list required a college degree. Self-employment, technical training, and apprenticeships are just a few of the ways used to circumvent the high cost and time commitment of college.

But What If I Don't Want to Go to College, by Harlow Unger
General availability
Cost: $10.95

> Lists eleven types of alternative education available.

Career Pathways
Available through Christian Financial Concepts
601 Broad St. SE, Gainesville, GA 30501 (800) 722-1976
Cost: $99.00

> After filling out an extensive questionnaire related to your talents and interests, you will receive an evaluation that suggests suitable jobs and provides you with the reasons for those suggestions.

What Color is Your Parachute?, by Richard Nelson Bolles
General availability
Cost: $14.95

> Help for the person trying to determine which job or career is most suitable for him.

HELPFUL BOOKS AND RESOURCES FOR PARENTS

The following books are available through general home-school mail-order catalog companies. See Appendix B for the contact information.

Help With Finding Available High School Curriculum

The Christian Home Education Curriculum Manual for Junior/Senior High, by Cathy Duffy
General availability
Cost: $19.95
> Excellent information on setting up your high school program and thorough reviews on available curriculum.

The Big Book of Home Learning - Volume 3, by Mary Pride
General availability
Cost: $25.00
> Reviews available high school curriculum and includes information and tips for setting up a program.

Help With Record Keeping and Creating Diplomas and Transcripts

Home School, High School, & Beyond: A Guide to Home Schooled Teens and Their Parents, by Beverly Adams-Gordon
Cost: $17.95
> A student-directed time management program that begins with goal setting, defines terms such as credits, transcript, etc. and then helps them choose their necessary courses geared to their future plans. Reproducible forms included.

Senior High: A Home-Designed Form+U+La, by Barbara Shelton
Cost: $24.95
> A step-by-step formula to personalize a master plan for your student. Especially useful for those seeking a less conventional approach. Reproducible masters included. Emphasizes seeking God's will for your teen and allowing Him to write the Master Plan.

Homeschooling the High Schooler, Volumes 1 and *2*,
by Diana McAlister and Candice Oneschak
Cost: $15.00 each volume
>*Volume 1:* goal setting, contracting between parent and teen, general information on how to design your own courses and then how to document it, and how to get into college.
>*Volume 2:* detailed information on designing your course of study (via conventional or non-conventional) with recommended resources.

Relaxed Record Keeping, by Mary Hood
Cost: $5.00.
>Written by the author of *The Relaxed Home School.* A brief account (27 pages) of how to comply with your law while relaxing your record-keeping style. She deals with educational objectives, journaling, creating a portfolio, high school and college considerations, and year-end assessment reports. She gives plenty of examples from her own journal to help you understand her method. A creative approach with no forms necessary.

Help With Apprenticeship

Apprenticeship Plus, by Inge Cannon
Available through Education Plus
Cost: $65.00
>Nine-hour seminar with 135-page notebook on apprenticeship and other topics concerning high school.

Family Testimonials

College Admissions: A Guide for Homeschoolers, by Judy Gelner
Cost: $7.95
>Hear how this family took the unschooling approach and how their son was still accepted at every college to which he applied.

Homeschooling for Excellence, by David and Micki Colfax
Cost: $10.99
>Don't miss this one! True "self-education" takes place in this family and Harvard and Yale are the result.

Help With Seeking College Acceptance and Finding Money For College

Bear's Guide to Finding Money for College, by John Bear
Cost: $7.95

Scaling the Ivy Wall: 12 Winning Steps to College Admission,
by Greene, Howard and Minton
Cost: $12.95

Peterson's Guide to Christian Colleges, by Thomas Hayden
Cost: $12.95

National Magazines For Teens

Brio (Teen girls) & *Breakaway* (Teen guys),
by Focus on the Family
Cost: $15.00 (Monthly)
Focus on the Family, P.O. Box 35500,
Colorado Springs, CO 80935

Chapter Eight

---•◆•---

Legalities, Record-Keeping and Achievement Testing

The question of legality is probably at the top of the "Most Frequently Asked Homeschool Questions" list. I still find that many people fear that home educating their children means they will be breaking the law and they will have to live in fear of being hauled off to jail or worse, have their children taken from them. You may have heard the horror stories of the first generation homeschoolers and unfortunately, we occasionally hear of current horror stories. However, let me assure you, because of the hard work and courage of those veteran homeschooling families, all 50 states now have laws to provide for the home education of your children, virtually free from the fears mentioned above.

Complying With Your State's Requirements

I wish I could inform you of your legal responsibilities with a simple national standard guideline. However, state's rights being what they are, each state has adopted their own law and requirements. It is very important that you become familiar with your state's law. Make it a priority to contact your state organization (see Appendix A). They can give you the information you are seeking and put you in contact with a local support network. If necessary you can go to your library and study your state's statutes for yourself. Remember, if you contact your local school board to inquire about regulations or requirements, I would caution you to check their advice or documents against the actual law. Many school districts have been known to ask for information which you are not required to reveal. It would be wise to contact a local support network (this can be accomplished through your state organization) and ask a knowledgeable person how the law is interpreted in your district. We have found in Florida that some counties are very homeschool friendly while others tend to harass and try to intimidate homeschoolers into complying with unlawful demands. You may also find that a surface reading of your state law appears confusing or difficult to follow while in actuality it is an easy matter with which to comply. Don't give up until you are confident you have the correct information. The bottom line here is to know your legal rights. There is freedom in knowing that if you follow the law then the law will also protect you.

OTHER LEGAL OPTIONS:

ENROLLMENT WITH A PRIVATE SCHOOL UMBRELLA OR SATELLITE SCHOOL

Many homeschooling families have found local or out-of-state Christian, parochial, or private schools that are willing to act as the overseer of their home education program. The school becomes the "umbrella" or legal covering, and the homeschool is then considered a "satellite" of that school. Check with your state homeschool regulations first to find out if this is a viable alternative. It would be best to check with your state or local support network as public schools may, knowingly or not, give you misinformation.

Whether local or out-of-state you should be prepared to follow all of their regulations plus pay any fees required. Many of the correspondence schools offer this umbrella, however, you need to see if any particular accreditation affiliation is necessary for your needs. Many schools are accredited under associations which are not recognized or accepted by some states or organizations. For most homeschoolers that won't matter. However, some families need proper accreditation to meet requirements for involvement in particular organizations. For example: a young lady in our city was a competitive swimmer and was required to adhere to NCAA rules. One rule was that her high school courses had to be accredited through an acceptable accreditation association. If you find this necessary for your child see Appendix B for the contact information for "Correspondence Schools" and "School Services."

Noncompliance: Standing On Your U.S. Constitutional Rights

This option is for those families who do not desire to register under their state homeschool law. These families must maintain a "lifestyle conviction" that upholds the belief that parents have the sole responsibility under God, and the freedom provided them under the United States Constitution, for raising and educating their children without any state intervention or compliance with any state regulations. These parents believe that the United States Constitution covers them legally under their first amendment rights to freedom of religion.

I spoke to a few families who are doing this and I will pass along to you what they believe are the advantages and disadvantages to this.

Advantages of Noncompliance

1. This satisfies the consciences of those parents who feel it is their religious and/or moral obligation to refrain from any entanglement with the state.
2. The parents will not need to keep any state-mandated documentation. (However, steps to document the educational process are recommended to be taken for use in court if ever needed.)

DISADVANTAGES OF NONCOMPLIANCE

1. Children of compulsory attendance age who are not attending a state approved form of education are generally considered truant. Noncompliance allows for the real possibility of a court proceeding and/or some form of penalty.
2. While you will not need to keep any state-mandated documentation, you may find it necessary to keep even more detailed documentation in the event you are ever confronted with a court hearing. It may be necessary to "prove" that an adequate education is occurring within the home.
3. One parent says that she feels more fearful than if she were complying with the law. She has found herself limiting their activities because she fears being detected and reported to the officials.

ADVICE FOR THOSE NOT COMPLYING

Some of the families I interviewed highly recommended seeking the counsel and/or the services of either The Rutherford Institute or The Home School Legal Defense Association (HSLDA) if you choose to homeschool under this option (see Appendix A). Should you need their services, these legal associations are willing to defend you based on your constitutional rights. Experience has shown that the strongest case for noncompliance is your ability to prove that your choice is based on a deep, religious conviction and not simply a preference. The courts do have a test to determine whether you have a "preference" or a "conviction."

The following information was submitted by a parent who has chosen not to register her children with the state or any institution. It is included to help you to determine whether this option is for you. Please consider the following:

1. Determine whether home education without state regulation is a conviction or a preference for you and your family. A *preference* is a very strong belief, but it is a belief you will change

under enough pressure from : a) peers, b) family, c) lawsuit, d) jail, or e) loss of physical life. A *conviction* is a belief that you will NOT change because it is a part of your very purpose, not something you have discovered along the way.

2. This option is not for those who are fearful. If you are called to this option, you will not fear.

3. This option does not mandate documentation of hours or of work done by students. However, for your personal integrity, it is highly recommended that you be able to document your child's education in some manner.

4. This option requires that its families have an understanding of the U.S. Constitution and of how it overrules state laws that are in direct conflict with it. State laws must be constitutional. All bills and statutes made by the state affect ONLY those who have chosen FREE PUBLIC EDUCATION. If you are teaching in the privacy of your home in the United States of America, under the direction of your spiritual authority, then these bills and statutes do not affect you. In conclusion, remember that freedom is NOT the ability to do as we please, but rather the opportunity to do what is right.

I extend my thanks to this parent for her willingness to share this information with others. It is her wish to remain anonymous.

In Summary

When deciding which option is most suitable for you, be careful to base your selection on what will meet the needs of your specific family. If possible, speak to other homeschooling families and find out their reasons for their selections.

Choosing Your Record-Keeping Style

Keeping records is an important habit for any homeschool family. Choose the most comfortable style of record keeping that will not only fulfill the law but also meet your needs based on factors such as time, number of children and degree of dedication to filling out your record book. Unless your state requires you to fill out and send in a particular set of forms, you should feel free to explore different approaches.

Some states require only a list of book titles and sample material with no mention of attendance, page numbers, or daily subjects while others require all of the above and more. When we began homeschooling the teacher in me longed to fill out all the little blocks of a "real" lesson plan book. (These can be purchased in most any parent/teacher school supply store or I have provided something similar in Appendix D.) Personally, I began to feel plagued by the empty squares that appeared since our school does not operate on the notion of having to teach every single subject every single day; not to mention the tedious and time consuming effort required. It might be O.K. for only one child (as when I first began) but the addition of children to our family excluded that option when I felt like I was spending as much or more time record keeping as I was teaching. I now have adopted a less rigid style of maintaining our records.

Forms have been provided in Appendix D to help you choose your method of record keeping. You may copy them as they are or use correction fluid to revise and reconstruct them into what will best suit your needs. These are only suggestions and not mandatory forms! If you have a different system which still complies with your state's law, I encourage you to use it.

Whatever method you choose, I would suggest you make entries at least on a weekly basis. Take it from experience; if you wait too long between entries you will forget many of the spontaneous "goodies" that are well worth mentioning.

RECORD-KEEPING RESOURCES

The following are some other sources that may help you keep your records. Unless otherwise indicated, each item listed here is available through most of the general homeschool mail order catalog companies. To contact these companies refer to Appendix B.

About the daily journal...
"It demonstrates system, helps in the ability to write, and is an excellent record."
— Dr. Raymond and Dorothy Moore, *Home Style Teaching*

Relaxed Record Keeping, by Mary Hood
Cost: $5.00.
> Written by the author of *The Relaxed Home School*. A brief account (27 pages) of how to comply with your law while relaxing your record-keeping style. She deals with educational objectives, journaling, creating a portfolio, high school and college considerations, and year-end assessment reports. She gives plenty of examples from her own journal to help you understand her method. A creative approach with no forms necessary.

The Home Education CopyBook!, by Katherine von Duyke
Cost: $25.00
> Page after page of reproducible forms for organizing your home and school including forms for the unit study approach. Adaptable for any teaching method because you pick and choose which forms are right for your family. Kathy goes into great detail on how to write educational objectives for those needing to do so for legal compliance. A great value considering you can use it year after year.

A Garden Patch of Reproducible Homeschooling Planning and Educational Worksheets, by Debora McGregor
Debora McGregor or Lifetime Books and Gifts
Cost: $25.00
> Includes planning and logging charts, portfolio and journaling forms, calendars, schedules, reports, evaluations, report cards, and award sheets. Also gives directions and provides forms to develop your portfolios, life notebooks, and history timelines.

Home School, High School, & Beyond, by Beverly Adams-Gordon
Cost: $17.95
> Helps your high schooler set up a student-directed time management program that begins with setting goals and provides the necessary forms with which to keep a complete portfolio of his achievements.

Senior High: A Home-Designed Form+U+La, by Barbara Shelton
Cost: $24.95

A very detailed record keeping and portfolio system for high schoolers. Among the many reproducible pages, Barbara includes samples and blank masters for transcripts and diplomas.

MORE ABOUT RECORD-KEEPING

It is not necessary to teach every subject every day. You just need to teach it often enough to insure adequate education and progression is made during the year. The pace should depend upon your child's readiness. But, what if your state requires an actual attendance and/or hourly record? Don't let this worry you. Homeschooling affords you the opportunity to view education beyond the parameters of the desk and classroom. With this in mind, almost all your child's waking hours can be considered legitimate "attendance" in your school. Did you help your child sound out words from billboard or traffic signs (phonics, reading) on the way to the grocery store (consumer math)? An afternoon street hockey game (phys. ed.) may follow a visit to the library (language arts). Your child's participation in preparing the evening meal could include following a recipe (language arts and math) and discussing a healthy meal (health and nutrition). The evening family devotional (religious or Bible instruction) may be followed by Dad reading aloud the next chapter of *Little House in the Big Woods* (history and language arts). Do you see what I mean? A significant amount of learning and practical application takes place during these times. With the inclusion of these hours you will be able to meet any state's hourly requirements with ease.

Many parents are concerned that they may not be teaching the appropriate subjects for their child's grade level. Remember to follow your child's readiness as your foremost guide. Beyond that, you should be able to obtain a list of your school district's or state's skills list of objectives from the local school, school board office, or your state's Department of Education. If you have trouble locating this, you can order the 50¢ booklet from World Book titled *Typical Course of Study: Kindergarten Through Grade 12*, by William Nault. Another source written by a home educator,

To be organized is not synonymous with meticulous. To be organized means you do things for a good reason at the best time and in the easiest way. It doesn't mean you never get behind, rather that you can stick to it until you have recovered.

— Bonnie McCullough, *Totally Organized*

Robin Scarlata, is called *What Your Child Needs to Know When* ($15.95). This resource lists objectives and skills that reflect what they will need to know to pass any of the major standardized achievement tests.

SAMPLE MATERIALS

Another seemingly universal requirement in states' laws is the parent's maintenance of sample materials for each child. As a homeschool evaluator I have seen many ways of keeping sample materials. I've seen methods all the way from a large box with everything in it including baseball and bowling trophies to file folders with just a few samples of work from the beginning, middle, and end of the school year. Check your law to see if there are any stipulations as to how elaborate yours must be.

Personally, I have found a 3-ring binder with pocket dividers (available at any office supply store) very helpful in this task. I label each pocket with the subjects we are covering: English, Spelling, Handwriting, Math, Social Studies, Science, Fine Arts, and Miscellaneous. Each day I simply deposit their work in the front of the appropriate pocket with the most recent work on top. The older children do this themselves to learn to keep their own records. I use as many pockets as necessary to compensate for the quantity of work. At the end of the year I have all their work together without a desperate, mad scramble to find something, anything, to show to the appropriate authority. If I only need to present a sample I can use a separate notebook and pull a few papers from the beginning, middle, and end of the school year which shows that progress is being made. I have found that this method prevents loose file folders from sliding around and spilling their contents all over the place.

Whatever method you adopt to keep your sample materials just remember they should be kept in chronological order for ease in showing progression in education.

Another nice addition to your portfolio is a photo album. Many families are using a more hands-on approach to their schooling and less paper work. When there are no papers to file, these photos will be sufficient to show that your child was involved in a creative activity or attended a field trip.

If your child is too young or not ready for writing assignments, allow your child to dictate to you. Keep these papers in the child's folder.

ELABORATE PORTFOLIO VS. BRIEF PORTFOLIO

This issue must be answered according to what is specifically required by your law. However, I don't think your portfolio should become a noose around your neck or a major time consumer. After all, you will want to get on with the reason for home educating your child in the first place — education!

Here are some of the arguments for and against elaborate and brief portfolios.

1. If you are required to have your child evaluated at the end of the year, the more elaborate portfolio may aid the teacher in determining the progress your child made. On the other hand, the evaluator may not require or even want elaborate documentation because it does take longer to wade through the material. I suggest contacting an evaluator at the beginning of the year to find out what that evaluator will want to see at the end of the year.
2. If a school official is required to inspect your portfolio and it is extensive, you may be relieved to be able to show him/her that a fully-developed home education program is taking place. A brief portfolio may be considered unsatisfactory. If this is the case, then make sure you are keeping the minimum requirements and then prepare for a possible struggle to preserve your rights.
3. If you ever consider entering your child into a public or private school, more elaborate documentation may be all that is required by a principal or headmaster to provide credits for subjects completed. Otherwise, placement tests and possibly even retention in a grade level could be the result. However, some principals have been known to ignore even the most elaborate and professional documentation and still require placement tests. If this should concern you, I would advise

you to check with the particular school you are considering and ask them what they require for a homeschooler to enter their program. In addition, one school official in my state even hinted at the fact that good documentation might someday be a means to authorize credits toward a diploma from the public system.

4. If, by chance, you become involved in a court proceeding challenging your homeschool program, a more elaborate portfolio may convince a judge that you are a responsible parent/teacher. Minimal documentation may give the appearance of a negligent parent/teacher.

5. Looking back on your documentation may give you a real sense of accomplishment when you ask yourself, "Did I really cover enough material this year?"

6. Elaborate to semi-elaborate documentation can be used as ready-made lesson plans for younger siblings as they get older.

7. Your record books may someday rank right up there with all the trophies, Boy Scout uniforms, and photo albums that you enjoy reminiscing over.

8. An elaborate portfolio takes more time and energy to compile which takes time and energy away from educating the child. It may cause unwarranted fear and stress on the parent to "perform" and this usually filters down to the child. Parents may begin to ask for more paper work activities from the child just to have something to put in the folder when a more hands-on approach would normally be used. This commonly leads to burnout for both the parent and the child (read *The Successful Homeschool Family Handbook*, by Dr. Raymond and Dorothy Moore, $13.00). The brief portfolio takes a minimal amount of time and leaves more time for educational activities.

9. The brief portfolio would be less likely to set a dangerous precedent in causing an evaluator or school official to expect elaborate documentation from all homeschoolers when the law does not specifically call for it.

Examination of some of the pros and cons of the two extremes seems to make a great case for a portfolio that might be called semi-elaborate. In whatever manner you keep your portfolio remember that it is an extension of your personality and style and should not be allowed to become an undue burden. Experiment and find the correct approach for YOU.

STANDARDIZED ACHIEVEMENT TESTS

Standardized Achievement Tests (also referred to as Nationally Normed Student Achievement Tests) are often required by states. Some of the more common test names are the **Iowa Tests of Basic Skills** (ITBS) for grades K-8, the **Stanford Achievement Test** (SAT) for grades K-12, the **California Achievement Test** (CAT) for grades K-12, the **Metropolitan Achievement Test** (MAT) for grades K-12, the **Comprehensive Test of Basic Skills** (CTBS) for grades K-12, and **The Tests of Achievement and Proficiency** (TAP) for grades 9-12. Some children affectionately call these the "bubble tests." (You probably remember, with some disdain, filling in those answer bubbles for the multiple-choice questions.)

The selection of which test can be used will most likely be determined by the school district in which you live. You should check with your school district or a local support group leader before you make a decision on which test to administer. Another consideration is whether you or someone else must administer the test. There may be certain qualifications such as state teacher's certification.

If you haven't heard about it yet, there is quite a controversy over standardized testing. Is it good or bad, detrimental or enriching, an effective indicator of a child's abilities or an unreliable indicator? Such is the nature of the standardized testing argument. As a testing administrator to homeschoolers since 1984, I believe it is safe to say that all of these qualities are apparent at least a portion of the time, some to a greater degree than others. Each year I find myself wrestling with the pros and cons. I have many misgivings about this form of evaluation. However, so many are legally bound by state laws to administer a standardized test that for now it is an issue that must be addressed and it is important to find ways to make the test more palatable to your child and the most beneficial to you.

Standardized testing is simply a test given under a standard of conditions (precise directions and time limits), with carefully cho-

Education is what survives when what has been learned has been forgotten.
— B.F. Skinner

157

sen test items, which report scores as percentiles, grade equivalents, and/or stanines. Preparing your child for the test includes helping your child to understand and experience the test conditions in a simulated fashion. The best way to do this is by using a practice test (see "Practice Test Distributors" later in this chapter).

Purchase your practice test as early in the school year as possible so you can familiarize yourself with the testing terminology and procedures and then integrate these into your homeschooling day. There are so many children who get hung up on terminology and miss simple items. For example, the mathematical term "rename" is just another term for borrow, carry, or regroup. If the test uses the term "rename" and your child has never seen the word before, he is lost, even though he may know the answer with the use of a different word.

Although you are purchasing the practice test early, you should not administer it until about two weeks before the formal standardized test. The practice test will not give you grade equivalents or percentiles but it will let you know where your child is struggling. Best of all, it will give your child practice with the testing *procedure* which is equivalent to a big dose of confidence on testing day.

While preparing your child for the actual test direct him to:

1. Read all test directions carefully.
2. Look for clue words.
3. Raise his hand (if in a group setting) and ask for help with directions if needed.
4. Answer all the questions he knows first.
5. Don't spend too much time on one item. Move on!
6. If time permits, go back to questions he isn't sure about and narrow down answers to make a logical guess.
7. If your child will be transferring answers to an answer sheet direct him to match the item numbers very carefully.
8. Use any extra time to check answers. If not sure, stick with the first choice.
9. Guess on a question rather than leaving it blank. (Check with your test administrator to be sure this is true for the test your child will receive. College entrance exams are the big exception.)

10. Only mark one answer bubble or it will be counted wrong.
11. Erase all errors and stray marks fully.
12. Use only a number 2 pencil if the test will be machine scored.
13. Do his best!

Here are some other test taking strategies that you can help your child with:

1. Help your child to learn how to pay attention, follow directions, and concentrate. Playing games of all types will build this skill.
2. Especially for young children: Teach them how to follow directions. Use direction words in your everyday language and make up games with words like start, stop, every, all, each, missing, matches, now, over, under, before, after, first, last, different, beginning, end, etc.
   A word of caution: If you have another evaluation option available for young children (K-2nd grade) besides standardized testing, perhaps a personal evaluation, I strongly advise opting for it.
3. Make sure your child is well-fed and well-rested on the testing day.
4. Build feelings of confidence in your child rather than anxiety. (Mom, you can be anxious enough for both of you.)
5. Stimulate your child to earnest effort.
6. Build math facts speed. A low score in a "Math Computation" test will markedly lower the "Total Math" average score.
7. Boost vocabulary by knowing common prefixes, suffixes, and roots. This allows the child to make a well-educated guess, if necessary.
8. Prepare your child for the environment he will be tested in especially if it will be a large group situation.

Now, when the test is over and you receive the scores, you may not know what the numbers mean. It is really no mystery that only the "professionals" can read. Here is a quick crash course in:

Understanding The Numbers

First, the scoring system is set up so that your child's raw score (number correct) is compared to the original group of students of the same age who first took the test. The averages of this original group are called the norms. Norm-referenced test scores compare your child's raw score to the norm group.

Next, your child's raw scores are converted into percentiles, grade equivalents, and stanines. Sometimes you will receive only one or two of these categories.

Percentiles: Let's say your child receives a 75% (read percentile). This means that if there were 100 kids taking the test, he did as well as or better than 75% of those kids in the norm group. It does *not* mean he got 75% of the items correct. Percentiles run from 1-99. There is not a 100 percentile because that would mean there were 101 kids in the norm group. A child cannot do better than 100 of the kids if he is number 100 because he can't do better than himself.

To rank percentiles qualitatively one might say that your child is having *great difficulty* with a skill if he only achieves a 1 - 10 percentile. He is having *difficulty* if he falls within the range of 10 - 30 percentile. His understanding of a skill is *somewhat below average* if he falls between 30 and 40 percentile. He has *average understanding* of a skill if the percentile is between 40 and 60. *Good understanding* falls between 60 and 75 percentile while *very good understanding* is between 75 and 90 percentile. Finally, he is considered to have an *excellent understanding* of a skill if his percentile ranking is between 90 and 99.

Grade Equivalent: If your child receives a 54 on an item it should be read as 5.4 or 5th grade, 4th month. Take caution here! This is the most misleading type of score. If your 2nd grader gets a 5.4 it does not mean your child is ready for 5th grade. It just means that an average 5th grader would have scored as well on the same test. It also lets you know that your 2nd grader mastered her material very well and answered most of the questions correctly.

Stanine: This term comes from the combination of the words *standard* of *nine*. It rates your child's achievement on a scale from 1-9 based on a coarse grouping of the percentiles. In general, a stanine of 1, 2, or 3 indicates below average achievement. A stanine of 4, 5, or 6 indicates average achievement while 7, 8, or 9 indicates above average achievement.

Of all the numbers explained above, the percentile ranking seems to be the truest indicator of how your child compares to others in the norm group and whether or not your child is having difficulty with a particular skill.

Now, how can all of this be of benefit to you or your child? My opinion is that the best thing to use these scores for is to find your child's strengths and weaknesses. This is easy to determine by looking at the percentiles. Praise your child for the strong areas and work on the weak areas. There may be areas which you have not even covered because you didn't realize it was a basic skill. The scores can help you choose remedial curriculum for the following school year.

Everything is great if your child scores relatively high and you feel pleased with your child's progress. But, what do you do when your child scores low? What does it mean and how should you react? A low score can mean the child simply didn't remember what he was taught or maybe you had never taught the material that was tested. Maybe you didn't feel the child was ready for some of the material. One major problem with this type of evaluation is that it does not take into account the readiness philosophy which so many of us adhere to.

Of course, there is always the possibility your child is a poor test taker. I had this difficulty during my school years. I would do extremely well in the classroom but would freeze on standardized tests. If your child falls into this category try to find an alternative form of evaluating, if possible. However, if your child is college bound, you will want to continue to teach your child test taking skills and try the standardized test again sometime. Like it or not, these are the types of tests your child will see for college entrance and he needs to know what he is doing.

Another area worth examining to explain low scores is the particular circumstances on the test day. Was your child sick or upset about family problems or was there an undue amount of test anxiety? Sometimes it is very easy for us as moms to put too much pressure on the children, even if we don't intend to. Many moms, myself included, feel that we are being evaluated more than our children.

I think most importantly, when reacting to low scores, we need to remember that the scores have nothing to do with a child's innate worth. Your reaction, positive or negative, will influence your child's sense of self-worth and anxiety on future tests. Assure your child that you will try to find out the reason for the low score and will help to improve the weak areas. Be sure to include praise for the strong areas.

Remember, you are the best judge of what your child knows. Your evaluation of this, coupled with the test results will give you a more complete knowledge of your child's abilities.

PRACTICE TESTING

Many parents have found that practice tests have eased the stress related to test taking. The practice test will familiarize your child with the test-taking process and some of the educational terms that you may not normally use. A few months prior to the test date you (without the child) should go through the practice test to look for those unfamiliar terms and procedures and include them in your curriculum. It is recommended that the practice test be administered no sooner than two or three weeks before the actual test date to allow the process to remain fresh in your child's mind.

PRACTICE TEST DISTRIBUTORS

1. Supplier of practice tests for ITBS, CAT, CTBS, MAT, and more:

   McGraw Hill / Scoring High Practice Tests
   (800) 843-8855

You must specify which test and what level you will need. Make sure you order the student book and teacher's book. These are very reasonably priced. No certification or approval is required.

2. Your public library contains resources which will help you to better understand and interpret standardized tests. Below are a couple of helpful ones.

   a. *The Parent's Handbook on School Testing*, by Ann Boehm and M.A. White 371.26 Bo or LB 3051.B58 in university libraries.
   b. Dr. Gary Gruber's *Essential Guide to Test Taking for Kids: Grades 3, 4, and 5*, 371.26 Gr in city libraries. (A separate book with the same title is available for grades 6, 7, and 8. This book is written for parents.)

OBTAINING A TEST

Unfortunately, obtaining a test can be a difficult process because many test suppliers sell exclusively to schools. The reason for this is to maintain strict security concerning availability, because over-availability can dilute the validity of a test. Check with your local support group to see whether group or individual testing will be conducted. Some public schools provide testing for homeschoolers along with their students. Another option is to check with local private schools to see if your child can test with them.

TEST DISTRIBUTORS

The following is a list of sources that will sell to individuals if you meet their criteria. You may request a free catalog from each one. Their catalog will describe their policies regarding who may order tests.

1. Supplier of ITBS, TAP, Cognitive Abilities Test (CogAt), Stanford Achievement Tests, and MAT Diagnostic Tests for grades K-12:

    Bob Jones University Press
    Testing Service
    Greenville, SC 29614
    (800) 845-5731

    BJU will only send the test to a qualified evaluator. You will qualify if you are a state certified teacher, a graduate of a four-year college, or a current teacher in a conventional school (not a homeschool). Your state may also have qualifications with which the evaluator must comply. Test materials must be sent back within 50 days. Scores will be sent to you within 4 to 7 weeks. The test prices vary and includes the fee for machine scoring, but not the price for the administrator. Perhaps you have a relative or friend you could ask to administer the test or check with your local support group for qualified administrators.

2. Supplier of CTBS:

    CTB McGraw Hill Order Service Center
    Del Monte Residential Park
    Monterey, CA 93940
    (800) 538-9547

    This will probably prove to be the hardest test to procure. You must obtain signed approval from a local or state school official. Tests are sold in packages of 35. A specimen kit containing one test is available, however, this will not include the scoring service or scoring masks.

3. Contact a local private school. Sometimes they will allow homeschoolers to take the tests along with their students or loan a test to a certified teacher to administer to your child on a private basis.

4. Contact your support group to find out if someone regularly administers a standardized test. It is possible that the person will allow a parent to borrow or rent a test if you meet their criteria.

CHAPTER NINE

---◆•◆•◆---

ANSWERS TO QUESTIONS FROM "WELL-MEANING" FAMILY AND FRIENDS

It is not unusual for uninformed or misinformed family members, friends, and even strangers in the grocery store to wonder, question, and criticize what you are doing. You might as well be prepared for their questions by having some answers for them.

My policy has always been to answer softly and without aggression or hostility. I immediately take the offensive approach by offering answers to other questions they haven't even asked or thought of yet. This prevents me from feeling like I have to defend myself or my beliefs. I know that if I can lead the conversation and keep it calm and rational, there will be a better chance of experiencing a favorable outcome.

When you discuss homeschooling with others, do not necessarily try to convince them you are right. Rather, use this as an opportunity to inform and educate. For each person that is properly informed, the homeschooling movement grows one step closer to being favorably accepted by today's society. Following are some typical questions from "well-meaning" family and friends — and some answers.

"WHY ARE YOU DOING THAT?"

The answers for why you are homeschooling will vary for each family. You may want to refer to the long-term goals you set for your children (see Chapter Four). Unless your reasons are too personal, be open with the inquirer and explain why homeschooling is a better option for your children.

The following are some of the common reasons why many parents choose to homeschool. However, not every family subscribes to all of them.

1. Strong conviction from the Lord that it is their scriptural duty to train up their own children in all aspects rather than surrendering them to strangers.

2. Feel the necessity to delay academics to allow the child to develop physically and emotionally. This is called "readiness" and is documented in *Better Late Than Early* and *School Can Wait*, by Dr. Raymond Moore.

3. Desire to avoid *negative* socialization (see a later discussion in this section).

4. Ability to move at the child's pace. The formal classroom moves at an average pace leaving the slow learner behind and failing to challenge the fast learner. (Read *The Hurried Child*, by David Elkind.)

5. Provides the opportunity to build foundational skills before formalized structure begins (see Chapter Six: "Preschoolers: Ages 4 and 5").

6. Provides the opportunity to instill solid character and moral values in the child so he will be more likely to stand against negative peer pressure.

7. Desire to create "thinkers rather than mere imitators of other people's thoughts." *

8. Opportunity to build a better sense of self-worth in the child.

9. Cannot afford to stay dependent on education that doesn't educate. (F.Y.I.: the illiteracy, dropout, and drug addiction rate is at an all time high in America. The teacher spends more time disciplining than educating. In the early 1800's children began public school between the ages of 8 and 12 and attended half days for three months each year. Literacy by the mid-1800's rose to 99%. In 1983, University of Texas determined that 20% of Americans do not have literacy survival skills i.e., the ability to sign a check, fill out an employment application, or complete a driver's license form. Another 30% have "doubtful" literacy survival skills.)*

10. Realization that the child in the home experiences 50 to 100 times as many personal adult to child responses as he would in a formal school. Schools give three or four responses per

child per day.*

11. Realization that the one-to-one tutorial method of teaching is a superior method and alleviates a lot of wasted time. It only takes one hour to teach at home what it takes six hours in a school. At home you avoid time wasted on administrative duties, classroom discipline, waiting on slower students, office interruptions, etc., etc.

    * Information and quotes are based on research by Dr. Raymond Moore.

When people ask you "why are you doing THAT?," do you ever feel they are implying that you are trying to "get out of something" or "get away with something?" They actually seem to insinuate that homeschoolers are somehow trying to shirk their duties or responsibilities. Assure them you will not be renting them out to migrant farmers. Believe it or not, this was actually a concern raised in the Florida legislature when our state law was being considered in 1985. Also, assure them that what you are doing requires much more responsibility and far greater sacrifices than if you merely dropped your child off at a school each day and picked him up again six hours later, having the day to yourself. Be careful with this one if you're speaking to someone who is doing just that. You may intimidate a friend.

"ISN'T THAT ILLEGAL?"

With your state homeschool law understood you can confidently tell them, "NO!"

"YOU'RE NOT A PROFESSIONAL, SO HOW CAN YOU TEACH?"

Oh, but yes, you are a professional! You are a professional parent who has completed at least five years of intensive training with the very child you will be educating. In fact, aren't you the very person who taught your child how to speak a language, how to tie his shoes and use a toilet? Aren't you the one who taught

> In a reasonably warm home, parent-child responses, the true ABC's of sound education, are likely to be a hundred times more frequent than the average teacher-child responses in a classroom.
> — Dr. Raymond and Dorothy Moore, *Home Style Teaching*

Socialization is actually the ability of one generation to communicate its values to the next. Homeschooling does this far better, simply by its structure.
— Kathy von Duyke

Most people these days tend to regard socialization as a random mixing of people without serious thought about the quality of the mixture.
— Dr. Raymond and Dorothy Moore, *Home Style Teaching*

him the alphabet, how to count to ten and distinguish between colors and shapes? Didn't you teach him personal grooming habits, how to dress, and how to eat politely? Maybe you've even done this several times over with many children. I'd say you qualify as a "pro."

Of course, they'll argue that they mean "trained as an educator." You should argue back (politely, of course) that there is no magic age when a parent should stop educating his child unless he comes to a point where he himself feels unqualified. Then, of course, there are tutors. After all, are the "trained professionals" showing a huge success at turning out educated children?

Sometimes this question is asked by friends who automatically assume that now you must think you are a better mother than they are. Their feelings could possibly stem from a sense of guilt because they instinctively recognize the potential of home education. However, you can not be responsible for their feelings unless you truly are acting in a haughty manner. Lovingly assure them that you do not think you are a superior mother, but you do maintain this is the best form of education for your children.

"WHAT ABOUT "SOCIALIZATION?"

Ahhh, the "S" word! Because this is probably the most frequently asked question, the myth that peer socialization is always positive needs to be dispelled. Reliable studies have proven this to be in error. The following quote by Dr. Raymond Moore is taken from a synopsis bulletin in 1984.

Socialization: We later became convinced that little children are not only better taught at home than at school, but also better socialized by parental example and sharing than by other little children. This idea was fed by many researchers from Tufts, Cornell, Stanford and California. Among the more prominent were (1) Urie Bronfenbrenner who found that a least up to the sixth grade, children who spend less of their elective time with their parents than their peers tend to become peer-dependent; and (2) Albert Bandura who noted that this tendency has in recent years moved down to preschool, which in our opinion should be avoided whenever good parenting is possible. Contrary to common beliefs, little children are not best socialized by other kids; the more persons around them, the fewer meaningful contacts.

We found that socialization is not neutral. It tends to be either positive or negative: (1) Positive or altruistic and principled sociability is firmly linked with the family - with the quantity and quality of self-worth. This is, in turn, dependent largely on the track of values and experience provided by the family at least until the child can reason consistently. In other words, the child who works and eats and plays and has his rest and is read to daily, more with his parents than with his peers, senses that he is part of the family corporation — needed, wanted, depended upon. He is the one who has a sense of self-worth. And when he does enter school, preferably not before 8 to 10, he usually becomes a social leader. He knows where he is going, is independent in values and skills. He largely avoids the dismal pitfalls and social cancer of peer dependency. He is the productive, self-directed citizen our nation badly needs. (2) Negative, me-first sociability is born from more peer group association and fewer meaningful parental contacts and responsibility experiences in the home during the first 8 to 12 years. The early peer influence generally brings an indifference to family values which defy parents' correction. The child does not yet consistently understand the "why" of parental demands when his peers replace his parents as his models because he is with them more.

Research shows that such peer dependency brings loss of (1) self-worth, (2) optimism, (3) respect for parents, and (4) trust in peers. What does this child have left to lose? So he does what comes naturally. He adapts to the ways of his agemates because "everybody's doing it," and gives parent values the back of his little hand. And... he has few sound values to pass on to the next generation.

It is interesting to note that recently a teacher remarked that socialization within the schools is strongly discouraged. The rea-

When we live habitually with the wicked, we become necessarily their victims or their disciples; on the contrary, when we associate with the virtuous we form ourselves in imitation of their virtues, or at least lose, every day, something of our faults."

—Agapet

son she cited was that it is too easy to lose control of the children in the classroom resulting in more time being spent disciplining than educating.

Another resource on socialization is **Will My Child Fit?**, by June B. Whatley ($9.95). She is a former homeschooler (her son graduated from homeschool and is now in graduate school). She has worked in the areas of juvenile probations and counseling. She strongly espouses the benefits of family socialization in the homeschool.

The most recent and largest study on homeschooling was just released in March, 1997. The study was commissioned by the Home School Legal Defense Association (HSLDA) and conducted by Dr. Brian Ray of the National Home Education Research Institute (NHERI). Within his study, Dr. Ray found that the average homeschool student has 5.2 outside activities each week. This will counter the protest from many that homeschooled children are put in "social strait-jackets" and do not have adequate opportunities for socialization. If you are interested in reading this entire study for the latest facts on homeschooling, contact NHERI (see Appendix A) and request the book, *Strengths of Their Own - Home Schoolers Across America: Academic Achievement, Family Characteristics, and Longitudinal Traits*, by Dr. Brian Ray, $19.95

"WHAT ABOUT SPORTS INVOLVEMENT AND EXTRA-CURRICULAR ACTIVITIES?"

It is a sad commentary on a society that places more emphasis on sports than on education and family development. Many ask this question as if this were more important than the academic excellence the child is receiving. They seem to feel sorry for our "deprived children." I always assure them that if we choose for our children to be involved in organized sports, then we can easily take advantage of the many Optimist leagues available through our city.

Concerning extracurricular activities, I'm always quick to delineate the many wonderful activities in which we participate through our local homeschool support group. This is another good reason to belong to a support group or to organize one of your own (see Appendix A).

"WHEN ARE YOU GOING TO EXPOSE YOUR CHILD TO THE REAL WORLD?"

As members of a homeschool family, your children are definitely more exposed to the real world than a child in a conventional school. The typical classroom consists of four walls, 30 - 40 agemates, and one authority figure. A child spends six hours a day, 180 days per year in this setting. In my opinion, an institutional setting is not exposure to the real world nor is it even preparation for exposure to the real world.

On the other hand, the homeschool environment, by its very nature, consists of real-world exposure on a daily basis. When your children go to the grocery store with you, they observe how you deal with a person who runs into your shins with a grocery cart. They observe how you respond to an angry check out clerk. They learn correct procedures for banking, shopping, cleaning a home, doing laundry, preparing meals, dealing with traffic, tending to elderly or disabled neighbors, and many other activities. They are observing true-life experiences with true-life people of different ages, races, genders, nationalities, and abilities. Once explained, you may be surprised at the number of people who will agree with you. Society has extremely misled the public to believe that the sterile institutional-type classroom is a more nourishing environment than the home. Simple common sense tells us otherwise.

"IS HOME SCHOOLING ACCREDITED SO YOUR CHILD CAN ATTEND COLLEGE?"

Any home educated child can attend college if he is so inclined. College entrance is typically based on the college entrance exam scores and a high school transcript. See Chapter Seven for all the information pertaining to this.

Ideas are meant to be handed down from generation to generation. One generation is responsible for the next — whoever is doing the planting of ideas. The parents, or teachers, or professors... — Edith Schaeffer, *Forever Music*

"Hmm, Do You Think I Could Do It, Too!!?"

As the questions progress and you give rational answers to clear up any doubts or misconceptions, you may begin to see the wheels turning and a certain sparkle in their eye. Congratulations! You may have just recruited your first homeschooler or at least a new supporter. Generally speaking, once people become informed, they begin to look at you and homeschooling in a different light. They may no longer perceive you to be a radical fanatic bucking the establishment. They may actually begin to encourage you and applaud your endeavors. Of course, there will always be those who will not agree or even try to understand your rationale. Don't take it personally. If nothing else, you certainly gave them some food for thought. One day they may see the merit of homeschooling based on what you took the time to calmly and lovingly share with them.

Recommended Resources

The Successful Homeschool Family Handbook: A Creative and Stress-Free Approach to Homeschooling, by Dr. Raymond and Dorothy Moore (1994)
General availability
Cost: $13.00
> Within this incredibly encouraging book you will find scores of studies that will not only give you the confirmation and confidence to homeschool but also the data you can use to defend your choice and thwart your critics (maybe even convince them).

Strengths of Their Own - Home Schoolers Across America: Academic Achievement, Family Characteristics, and Longitudinal Traits, by Dr. Brian Ray (1997)
Available through National Home Education Research Institute
Cost: $19.95
> This book reveals the results (with interpretations) of the largest and most current (March, 1997) study of homeschooling ever conducted.

Right Choice - Home Schooling, The, by Chris Klicka
General availability
Cost: $13.95
> Exposes the failure and dangers of the public school system and reveals how homeschooling is the answer for our children and our nation.

Will My Child Fit?, by June Whatley
General availability
Cost: $9.95
> Espouses the benefits of family socialization in the home-school.

EPILOGUE

---•◆•---

SIMPLIFYING EDUCATION... SIMPLIFYING LIFE

Simplify! It's a term we hear often these days. We witness large companies downsizing and families leaving the cities for rural America in greater numbers than ever before. Just what are we searching for? Jack and I believe people want to reduce the complexity of their lives and return to the basic essentials in an attempt to provide clarity of purpose. Although society as a whole tends to overcrowd and complicate every area of life, I think homeschoolers are extremely susceptible to this. There are those who are fearfully concerned because the State is watching, the grandparents are watching, and their peers are watching. More often than not, in their attempt to satisfy everyone else's expectations, they find themselves dissatisfied with their overcrowded lives and the stress it produces. Sadly, these families often give up on homeschooling, unaware of its potential to provide exactly what they are seeking.

Then there are those parents who have a genuine desire to provide their children with such a "well-rounded" education that they find themselves forever carting everybody, everywhere, for every imaginable extra-curricular activity, and this on top of six hours of desk time. The levels of tension and stress create monsters out of mommies and unintentionally send a message to the children that this is what life is all about. They fall into bed exhausted and are left wondering how they'll make it through tomorrow. I know!... I've been there! It's not a happy place!

The most destructive consequence is that relationships are neglected, taken for granted, or just plain avoided. We believe the solution to this confusion requires us to redefine our interpretation of success and then redirect our priorities. If our priority becomes the "school house" instead of the "home" we lose

> God did not call me to be successful. God called me to be faithful.
> — Mother Teresa

174

the real intent of the homeschool. We must nurture the home first; making it a haven for spiritual growth, peacefulness, security, acceptance, and satisfying relationships. Nurturing these elements necessitates spending time in the home with each other rather than living fragmented lives with everyone doing their own thing. Karey Swan, author of *Hearth and Home* (see Appendix C), is a model of creative homemaking. Her book reflects the many conversations we have had throughout the years. She was my inspiration to move beyond maintenance, toward a lifestyle that resists fragmentation and emphasizes relationships. It's a lifestyle that gives us the permission we need to slow down, relax, and enjoy the life God has given us. It allows us to pursue our interests and model a peaceful, satisfied life removed from stress and unnecessary worry. Karey is often asked how she finds time to move beyond the maintenance level of home-keeping to pursue her own interests which include cooking from scratch, quilting, soap making, gardening, and canning. Her answer is simply: "I stay out of the car!" She wisely consolidates her errands, music lessons, grocery shopping, etc., so she is able to spend more time at home.

The main benefit I have found in living a quiet, contented life at home is it allows me to model a Learning Lifestyle (see Chapter Three). By having the time and energy to pursue my interests in the home, the children are inspired by my enthusiasm to learn new things. When I become curious about something (such as gardening, canning, and freezing), I throw myself into it, read and learn all I can, and then apply my knowledge. Our children follow that pattern and are always involved in learning something based on their own curiosity and interest in a topic. This is in conjunction with their basic studies suited to their readiness and needs. In essence, this is simplified education.

Simplified education removes the complexities and reduces education to its basic essentials. We spend less time at the desk and much more time on the living application. This serves to give clarity of purpose to a child's learning. You may think this means I am proposing simplistic school work or laziness. Not at all! Ironically our children work harder at their "school" because they are, for the most part, pursuing their interests and are, therefore, motivated to learn. They only refer to their desk time as

A family is a formation center for human relationships... the place where the deep understanding that people are significant, important, worthwhile, with a purpose in life, should be learned at an early age. — Edith Schaeffer, *What Is a Family?*

"school." The rest, I suppose, they consider part of our lifestyle, even though that is where most of their worthwhile learning is taking place. They now spend more time reading than when I used to assign it *and* without any complaints (they still have assigned reading when it's warranted, however). They spend more time than ever before using critical thinking skills such as pondering, questioning, and discussing. Again, they are motivated by *their* curiosity rather than by *my* assignment. After all, what is the purpose of education if not to teach them how to learn on their own?

Simplified education provides the time and inspiration for every member of the family to pursue learning, just as "staying home" will provide the time for moving beyond maintenance in your home. If your children are burdened with hours of conventional-style education every day, you will all be too tired, and uninspired, to pursue the best part of learning — interest-based, self-education. Yes, you must teach the basics, but give your children the time, the freedom, and the permission to, at least sometimes, *apply those basics while studying their own topics of interest.*

Let me reiterate that this style of learning (referred to as the Learning Lifestyle) provides the clarity of purpose they need to make sense of what they are learning. Trust them! *Children will learn in spite of us and our concept of curriculum!* God has given them sufficient stores of wonder and awe to learn beyond the parameters of what many have come to define as "education." To suppress a child's natural love for learning is to do him a great injustice. It leads him away from true education, not toward it. I would challenge you to try it! Don't be scared! I know you'll be satisfied with the results. O.K., if you have to, tell yourself you are conducting a scientific experiment and are collecting comparative data. That sounds very educational, doesn't it? Just remember this takes time! It may take several months or an entire school year for everyone to complete the "withdrawal" process, especially for those children just coming out of a conventional school setting. You may suffer from panic attacks and a false sense of guilt because you'll feel as if you aren't doing enough. Beyond your assistance in teaching the basics, it shouldn't be you doing it anyway. Even some children will have to take time adjusting to self-education. Many are too satisfied with being fed predigested information since it requires little thinking on their part. Some children will express a genuine desire to use formal materials. Allow them to pursue learning in the manner that best gets the job done. It's O.K.! However, don't expect that just because your son wants to fill out a worksheet today means he wants to do it that way forever and ever, Amen!.

A simplified education promotes *integration* of all facets of life. It is relational in nature because your children will be conversing with you more and spending fewer hours filling out rote facts in workbooks. You will find that relationships will naturally be nurtured. For example: while a mother assists her daughter in sewing a dress, skills such as measurement, reading and following directions, coordination, and creativity are learned through application. Perhaps the daughter reveals a concern and asks her mom to help her think it through. This may be a particularly sensitive issue that would never have come up had they not spent an extended amount of time together. Here is an opportunity to help her daughter with logic and critical thinking skills plus the added advantage of working on a project that moves beyond typical home maintenance into an area of interest. But, the greatest aspect of this integration of activities is the relational benefits derived.

While this evokes the ideal, the reality in some families is daunting. Some have lived with fragmentation for so long, they have difficulty relating one to another. Fragmentation suggests a state of being incomplete — simply bits and pieces or scraps — merely parts which exist separate from the whole. For those families, developing and nurturing relationships may be the most difficult aspect of homeschooling. The good, the bad, and the ugly is confronted on a daily basis. Don't give up or be tempted to return to fragmentation. Give yourselves time, lots of time, to adjust and work through the problems and issues. Ask God to intervene and take the fragments of your family's lives and bind them together to provide a unified purpose. He cares about the fragments. After intervening to supply the multitude with food, Christ directed His disciples to, "Gather up the leftover fragments, that nothing may be lost" John 6:12. Fragments which are separated from the whole are easily lost. This is evidenced

Almost every worthwhile question about life will eventually come up if a parent and child spend enough time together.
— Jay Kesler, *Ten Mistakes Parents Make With Teenagers*

Minds that have nothing to confer find little to perceive.
—Wordsworth

177

by the scores of broken families throughout the world. Intact relationships require time and attention. Time spent together reading aloud, story-telling, playing games, sharing interests, having discussions over unhurried meals, and daily family devotions are just some of the ways we can build enduring relationships.

In order to live a simplified life, it becomes essential that we control the areas that sap our family's joy for living and learning. Many believe there is nothing they can do about the stress in their lives. They feel trapped, with no way out. We read a life-changing book which revealed the insidious culprit and gave practical tips for how to regain control. The title is ***Margin: Restoring Emotional, Physical, Financial, and Time Reserves to Overloaded Lives***, by Richard Swenson, M.D., $12.00 (see Appendix C). Dr. Swenson wrote this after witnessing the painful results of overloaded lives in himself and his patients. He concluded, people need to return "margin" in their lives.

Margin is the space that exists between us and our emotional, spiritual, physical, and financial limits. Margin allows us the freedom to deal with life's surprises and still maintain sanity. It guards us from overload and gives us permission to take the time needed to think and to heal. When we have no margin, our limits have been exceeded. We are then besieged by pain, stress, and overload. Imagine with me for a moment about margin. You know that one-inch of white, blank space around the body of a text? That white stuff makes us feel comfortable and is easier on our eyes and even more inviting to read. Imagine that same text page with small black letters starting at the very top, left-hand corner and covering the entire page down to the bottom, right-hand corner. Would that be very comfortable to read? Most of us wouldn't want to have anything to do with it. Now imagine you and your family are the text on the page and ponder this: Would you rather live on the page with no margin or the page with margin?

The page without margin leaves us with the feeling that we are teetering on the brink of destruction. One false move, the slightest addition to our lives, whether good or bad, such as work or church responsibilities, homeschooling, sickness, financial crisis, etc., would send us and our family over the edge. But, the page with margin gives us room to deal with unanticipated crises or God's unexpected call to do His bidding. It's the "elbow-room" we need for the times when a "big push" is required. Amazingly, the stress levels stay low because we are secure in the knowledge that we will soon draw back to the margin line — the line that restores the space to relax, to think, to heal, and to build relationships. From our personal experience, the longer we live with margin the less we are tempted to fill up the blank space. Margin is comfortable and rewarding and the protection of it becomes a priority. It is truly a wonderful place to be! If you read nothing else I've recommended, please read this book. It will reveal how we lose life's margin and then how to regain it.

While margin cannot give us any more hours in our day, it does, in effect, help us to redirect our priorities so our time is spent on the essential things. We must worship, learn, work, rest, eat, and nurture relationships through it all. Apportioning the correct amount of time to each is the tricky part. If we give too much time in one area we will neglect our duties in another. If we don't attempt to balance our lives then we lose the battle. To try and make up for it we often take short cuts. We don't like things that take too much time or require us to wait. That point slaps me in the face when I find myself tapping my foot while waiting for the microwave to heat up an instant cup of tea.

We've been conditioned through our "instant-mentality" society to believe the faster we can get something accomplished, the better. We want what we want, when we want it! Micro-waves and fast food restaurants give us instant food, tempting us to eat on the run, eliminating family meal-time gatherings. Television and computer screens give us instant entertainment, tempting us to be entertained by strangers rather than each other. Telephones give us instant communication, tempting us to make a quick call rather than write a letter that can be re-read and cherished long after the phone call ends. Phones have preyed upon the development of the gift of hospitality since a call is more convenient than a visit. Cars give us instant mobility, tempting us to go, go, go! Do I advocate getting rid of any of these things? No! I do, however, advocate controlling them and giving priority to that which is truly important. People should be considered more important than things.

Our modern conveniences can save our lives or we can allow

In the rush and noise of life, as you have intervals, be still. Wait upon God and feel his good presence; this will carry you evenly through your day's business.
— William Penn

Life-giving story
transcends facts.
Every time a
story is told well,
people get a sense
that life has value
and meaning,
that we are
significant.
Story gives us
context.
— Karey Swan,
*Hearth and
Home*

them to overload us, rob our joy, and even kill us if we allow stress to reach levels sufficient to cause heart attacks. We must spend time relaxing, thinking, and interacting with each other and our Maker. We must come to terms with living with simplicity, contentment, balance, and rest, advises Dr. Swenson. We must allow God to lead us beside the still waters and then we must be still in order to know the Author of peace.

Although progress has produced an "instant-mentality" society, it does not mean we have to surrender the things of worth... our imagination, our creativity, or our relationships. My precious, 87-year-old Grandma Askew has written hundreds of poems that recall the days of her youth in the hollow (pronounced "holler") in Tennessee. When I discussed this chapter with my mother she reminded me that Grandma had written a poem about this very subject. Grandma has managed to capture in six stanzas the very essence of what I have rambled on about for several pages. For as long as I can remember, Grandma has used story telling and the recitation of her poems to teach us about our rich family heritage. Those times together exercise our imaginations and train us in the art of listening. I am honored to be able to print her poem here because Grandma, and her love for genealogy and the relationships our ancestors represent, has always modeled the things of true value and worth. Thanks, Grandma!

THE INSTANT CUP

Reflecting on those olden days, before the "Instant Cup"
My mind recalled the coffee bean we ground before we supped.

Grandma Moses reflected her days with canvas and with brush;
While Papa told his day with simple little verse.

"Oh were you ne'er a school boy, and did you never 'train'
And feel that feeling in your heart you ne'er can feel again?"

Today's electric motors and computers
Have long replaced the child's "Riding Stick."
There's no need to want, nor improvise, there's "Instants" he can pick.

Has this "Instant Cup" mentality made our homes more happy and safe?
If so, why are our homes invaded and locks on every gate?

Things of worth have been discarded in our rush to fill our "cups"
Full of all this earth can offer while throwing out, "In God We Trust."

Ina Askew (1995)

Following is the first song I ever heard Monte and Karey Swan sing. They shared it one day with several friends, and I do believe there wasn't a dry eye in the house. This song captures what is truly important in life. To hear this song and more of their family-oriented music you can purchase their cassette tape, *True to You*, from Singing Springs Productions for $10.00. One listener describes it this way: "This album will minister and heal your tired heart, reminding you of all the values you are fighting for in your home: love of family, spouse, children, and a lifestyle that worships God." The Swans frequently perform their music and speak at homeschool conventions around the country. "Relationship" is their prevailing message!

THOSE WERE THE BEST DAYS

Her work seems to never end, and lately her days run together.
But she knows the page she'll write tonight, will last forever.
She listens for the little boy, who'll soon stand at her knee,
Holding up his story book he'll say, "Mommy, will you read to me."

Another day nearly done, he can settle down and read the news.
But then a sweet voice whispers his name, "Daddy, can I read with you."
He puts down his evening paper and draws his treasure near.
With his arm around his little girl, it all becomes perfectly clear.

A home's not a big house on a hill, it's not a picture in a magazine.
It's not two strangers with their kids, watchin' strangers on TV.
'Cause homes are built on dreams we share,
And homes are held together with bedtime prayers,
And that old-fashion family love.
And knowin' that Jesus cares. Mostly knowin' that Jesus cares.

Mamma teaches to the heart, and she's a model of hope and love.
Daddy protects his family with strength from the Lord above.
They know the house will soon be still, then they'll look back with smiles and say,
"Of all the times we spent on earth those were the best days."

A home's not a big house on a hill, it's not a picture in a magazine.
It's not two strangers with their kids, watchin' strangers on TV.
'Cause homes are built on dreams we share,
And homes are held together with bedtime prayers,
And that old-fashion family love.
And knowin' that Jesus cares. Mostly knowin' that Jesus cares.

— Monte Swan, (1991)

I suppose the time has come to close this book. Completing a book (whether I'm reading or writing it) always leaves me with a bitter-sweet feeling. It has been wonderful sharing my thoughts with you. I always fear, however, that in my zealous "philosophizing" I may intimidate someone. I hope that is not the case with you. I hope that instead you have been inspired.

If by chance our paths cross, give me a nod or a hug and whisper "cuppa" in my ear and I will be blessed to know that we have shared some kindred moments.

> ... Never a cup of tea large enough
> or book long enough...
> — C.S. Lewis

What are the good old days? What do they mean? What have we lost? Lord, what have we gained? Nostalgic days gone by. We dream and think we can. But do we yearn for what we'll never have? Or do we hold it in our hands?
— Monte Swan

And time seems to fly, oh, the years pass so quickly now,
Like sand through your fingers, you hold it once and then it's gone.
The children keep changing, they grow as the years rush by.
Like arrows in a quiver, they're made to someday fly.

— Monte Swan

It will be gone before you know it.
The fingerprints on the wall appear higher and higher.
Then suddenly they disappear.

— Dorothy Evslin, born 1923, American writer

In E.B. White's *Charlotte's Web*, Wilbur asks the dying spider what she is working on. The spider replies that she is working on her "magnum opus," her greatest work, her egg sac. We believe that our children are our magnum opus.

— Jessica Hulcy, KONOS Curriculum

APPENDIX A

---•◆•---

SUPPORT ORGANIZATIONS

YOUR STATE-WIDE SUPPORT GROUP

There are support groups for all kinds of organizations throughout America and homeschooling is no different. Homeschoolers have found strength and encouragement in unity. The number of support groups have grown considerably in the last few years.

Most state organizations began with the idea that their state legislature would be more likely to listen to the organized voice of many rather than varied opinions and appeals from individual homeschoolers throughout the state. They were right! During the 80's and early 90's state after state began adopting homeschool laws when the homeschoolers of each state presented a unified front and requested, even demanded in some cases, to be allowed to educate their own children free from the fear of legal retaliation. These same state organizations realized that even though the big battle was won, it would be necessary to keep an ever-watchful eye on each legislative session to insure unwanted changes weren't made.

Other functions of a state organization may include disseminating information via a state-wide newsletter, organizing a state-wide curriculum fair and conference and the general encouragement of their members. They can also put you in touch with other families or a support group in your local area.

State Support Organizations

Below you will find a listing of the major state organizations throughout the country. Many states have more than one group. Most likely that is because some are secular in nature while others are religious. Still others hold to Judeo-Christian beliefs yet open their membership to all homeschoolers regardless of race, religion, or creed. My recommendation is to interview the available organizations and find the group you feel most comfortable supporting. You should expect to pay some amount in dues to offset the many costs incurred in operating such an organization. There is strength, recognition, and power in numbers.

ALABAMA
Christian Home Education Fellowship of Alabama
P.O. Box 563, Alabaster, AL 35007
(205) 664-2232

ALASKA
Alaska Private & Home Educators Association
P.O. Box 141764, Anchorage, AK 99514
(907) 753-3018

ARIZONA
Arizona Families for Home Education
P.O. Box 4661, Scottsdale, AZ 85261-4661
(602) 443-0612

Christian Home Educators of Arizona
P.O. Box 13445, Scottsdale, AZ 85267-3445

Flagstaff Home Educators
6910 West Suzette Lane, Flagstaff, AZ 86001
(520) 774-0806

ARKANSAS
Arkansas Christian Home Education Association
Box 4025, North Little Rock, AR 71290
(501) 758-9099

CALIFORNIA
Christian Home Educators Association
P.O. Box 2009, Norwalk, CA 90651
(310) 864-2432 or (800) 564-CHEA

Family Protection Ministries
910 Sunrise Ave., Suite A-1, Roseville, CA 95661

COLORADO
Christian Home Educators of Colorado
3739 E. 4th Avenue, Denver, CO 80206
(303) 388-1888

Concerned Parents for Colorado
P.O. Box 547, Florissant, CO 80902

CONNECTICUT
The Education Association of Christian Homeschoolers
25 Fieldstone Run, Farmington, CT 06032

DELAWARE
Delaware Home Education Association
P.O. Box 1003, Dover, DE 19903
(302) 368-3427

Tri-State Home School Network
P.O. Box 7193, Newark, DE 19714
(302) 368-4217

DISTRICT OF COLUMBIA
Bolling Area Home Schoolers of D.C.
1516-E Carswell Circle, Washington, DC 20336

FLORIDA
Florida Parent-Educators Association
P.O. Box 371, Melbourne, FL 32902-0371
(407) 722-0895
e-mail: office@fpea.com
website: www.fpea.com

Florida Coalition of Christian Private School Administrators
5813 Papaya Dr., Ft. Pierce, FL 34982
(407) 465-1685

GEORGIA
Georgia Home Education Association
245 Buckeye Lane, Fayetteville, GA 30214
(770) 461-3657

North Georgia Home Education Association
200 West Crest Road, Rossville, GA 30741

Georgia for Freedom in Education
209 Cobb Street, Palmetto, GA 30268
(770) 463-3719

HAWAII
Christian Homeschoolers of Hawaii
91-824 Oama Street, Ewa Beach, HI 96706
(808) 689-6398

IDAHO
Idaho Home Educators
P.O. Box 1324, Meridian, ID 83680
(208) 323-0230

ILLINOIS
Illinois Christian Home Educators
Box 310, Mt. Prospect, IL 60056
(847) 670-7150

Christian Home Educators Coalition
P.O. Box 470322, Chicago, IL 60647
(312) 278-0673

INDIANA
Indiana Association of Home Educators
850 N. Madison Ave., Greenwood, IN 46142
(317) 859-1202

IOWA
Network of Iowa Christian Home Educators
Box 158, Dexter, IA 50070
(515) 789-4310 or (800) 723-0438

KANSAS
Christian Home Education Confederation of Kansas
P.O. Box 3564, Shawnee Mission, KS 66203
(316) 945-0810

KENTUCKY
Christian Home Educators of Kentucky
691 Howardstown Road, Hodgensville, KY 42748
(502) 358-9270

Kentucky Home Education Association
P.O. Box 81, Winchester, KY 40392-0081
(606) 744-8562

LOUISIANA
Christian Home Educators Fellowship
P.O. Box 74292, Baton Rouge, LA 70874-4292
(504) 775-9709

MAINE
Homeschoolers of Maine
HC62, Box 24, Hope, ME 04847
(207) 763-4251

MARYLAND
Maryland Association of Christian Home Educators
P.O. Box 247, Point of Rocks, MD 21777-0247
(301) 607-4284

Christian Home Educators Network
304 North Beechwood Avenue
Catonsville, MD 21228
(410) 744-8919 or (410) 444-5465

MASSACHUSETTS
Massachusetts Homeschool Organization of Parent Educators
5 Atwood Road, Cherry Valley, MA 01611-3332
(508) 755-4467

MICHIGAN
Information Network for Christian Homes
4934 Cannonsburg Road, Belmont, MI 49306
(616) 874-5656

MINNESOTA
Minnesota Association of Christian
Home Educators
P.O. Box 32308, Fridley, MN 55432-0308
(612) 717-9070

MISSISSIPPI
Mississippi Home Educators Association
109 Reagan Ranch Road, Laurel, MS 39440
(601) 649-6432

MISSOURI
Missouri Association of Teaching
Christian Homes
307 East Ash Street, #146, Columbia, MO 65201
(573) 443-8217

Families for Home Education
400 E. High Point Lane, Columbia, MO 65203
(417) 782-8833

MONTANA
Montana Coalition of Home Schools
P.O. Box 654, Helena, MT 59624
(406) 587-6163

NEBRASKA
Nebraska Christian Home Educators
Association
P.O. Box 57041, Lincoln, NE 68505-7041
(402) 423-4297

NEVADA
Home Education And Righteous Training
P.O. Box 42262, Las Vegas, NV 89116
(702) 391-7219

Northern Nevada Home Schools
P.O. Box 21323, Reno, NV 89515
(702) 852-6647

NEW HAMPSHIRE
Christian Home Educators
of New Hampshire
P.O. Box 961, Manchester, NH 03105

NEW JERSEY
Education Network of Christian
Homeschoolers
120 Mayfair Lane, Mount Laurel, NJ 08054
(609) 222-4283

NEW MEXICO
Christian Association of Parent Educators
of New Mexico
P.O. Box 25046, Albuquerque, NM 87125
(505) 898-8548

NEW YORK
Loving Education At Home
P.O. Box 88, Cato, NY 13033
(716) 346-0939

NORTH CAROLINA
North Carolinians for Home Education
419 N. Boylan Avenue, Raleigh, NC 27603
(919) 834-6243

NORTH DAKOTA
North Dakota Home School Association
4007 N. State Street, Route 5, Box 9
Bismarck, ND 58501
(701) 223-4080

OHIO
Christian Home Educators of Ohio
430 N. Court Street, Circleville, OH 43113
(614) 474-3177

Home Education Action Council of Ohio
P.O. Box 24133, Huber Heights, OH 45424
(513) 845-8428

OKLAHOMA
Christian Home Educators Fellowship
of Oklahoma
P.O. Box 471363 Tulsa, OK 74147-1363
(918) 583-7323

Oklahoma Central Home Educators
P.O. Box 270601, Oklahoma City, OK 73137
(405) 521-8439

OREGON
Oregon Christian Home Education Association Network
2515 N.E. 37th, Portland, OR 97212
(503) 288-1285

PENNSYLVANIA
Christian Home School Association of Pennsylvania
P.O. Box 3603, York, PA 17402-0603
(717) 661-2428

Pennsylvania Homeschoolers
R.D. 2, Box 117, Kittanning, PA 16201
(412) 783-6512

RHODE ISLAND
Rhode Island Guild of Home Teachers
P.O. Box 11, Hope, RI 02831-0011
(401) 821-1546

SOUTH CAROLINA
South Carolina Home Educators Association
P.O. Box 612, Lexington, SC 29071
(864) 754-6425

South Carolina Association of Independent Home Schools
P.O. Box 2104, Irmo, SC 29063
(803) 551-1003

SOUTH DAKOTA
Western Dakota Christian Homeschools
P.O. Box 528, Black Hawk, SD 57118
(605) 787-6319

TENNESSEE
Tennessee Home Education Association
3677 Richbriar Court, Nashville, TN 37211
(615) 834-3529

TEXAS
Home-Oriented Private Education for Texas
P.O. Box 59876, Dallas, TX 75229-9876
(214) 358-2221

Texas Home School Coalition
P.O. Box 6982, Lubbock, TX 79493
(806) 797-4927

North Texas Home Education Network
P.O. Box 59627, Dallas, TX 75229
(214) 234-2366

Family Educators Alliance of South Texas
4719 Blanco Road, San Antonio, TX 78212
(210) 342-4674

South East Texas Home School Assoc.
4950 F.M. 1960W Suite C3-87,
Houston, TX 77069
(713) 370-8787

UTAH
Utah Christian Homeschoolers
P.O. Box 3942, Salt Lake City, UT 84110-3942
(801) 296-7198

VERMONT
Christian Home Educators of Vermont
214 N. Prospect #105, Burlington, VT 05401
(802) 658-4561

VIRGINIA
Home Educators Association of Virginia
P.O. Box 6745, Richmond, VA 23230-0745
(804) 288-1608

WASHINGTON
Washington Association of Teaching Christian Homes
N. 2904 Dora Road, Spokane, WA 99212

Washington Homeschool Organization
18130 Midvale Avenue North,
Seattle, WA 98083

WEST VIRGINIA
Christian Home Educators of West Virginia
P.O. Box 8770, South Charleston, WV 25303
(304) 776-4664

WISCONSIN
Wisconsin Christian Home Educators
2307 Carmel Avenue, Racine, WI 53405
(414) 637-5127

WYOMING
Homeschoolers of Wyoming
339 Bicentennial Court, Powell, WY 82435
(307) 754-3271

INTERNATIONAL ORGANIZATIONS

CANADA
Alberta Home Education Association
Box 3451, Leduc, Alberta, T9E 6M2
(403) 986-4264

ENGLAND
Education Otherwise
36 Kinross Road, Leamington Spa, Warks,
ENGLAND, CV32 7EF
Tel. 0926 886.828

JAPAN
KANTO Home Educators Association
PSC 477 Box 45, FPO, AP 96306-1299

GERMANY
Eifel Area Home Schoolers
52 SPTG/MW, UNIT 3640 BOX 80
APO, AE 09126

Verna Lilly
PSC 118 Box 584, APO AE 09137
011 49 6561 5341

NEW ZEALAND
Christian Home Schoolers of New Zealand
4 Tawa Street, Palmerston North, New Zealand

PUERTO RICO
**Christian Home Educators
of the Caribbean**
Palmas Del Mar Mail Service, Box 888
Suite 273, Humacao, PR00791
(787) 852-5284

MILITARY
Christian Home Educators on Foreign Soil
Mike & Diane Smith, 1856 CSGP
PSC2 Box 8462, APO, AE 09012

SPECIALTY ORGANIZATIONS

NATHHAN
National Challenged Homeschoolers
Association Network
5383 Alpine Road, S.E., Olalla, WA 98359
(206) 857-4257

Jewish Home Educators Network
c/o Emstoff
2 Webb Road, Sharon, MA 02067

**National Association of
Catholic Homeschoolers**
P.O. Box 420225, San Diego, CA 92142

**Single Parents Educating Children
in Alternative Learning**
2 Pineview Drive, #5, Amelia, OH 45102

Home Education Radio Network
P.O. Box 3338, Idaho Springs, CO 80452
(303) 567-4092

revised 2/10/97
Courtesy of HSLDA

NATIONAL SUPPORT ORGANIZATIONS

THE RUTHERFORD INSTITUTE (TRI)

The Rutherford Institute was founded in 1982 by John W. Whitehead, a recognized specialist in constitutional law. The Rutherford Institute specializes in cases pertaining to our First Amendment rights, specifically religious freedoms, free exercise and free speech. This is a Christian-based organization but they are dedicated to intervening and/or litigating on behalf of anyone whose First Amendment rights are being violated regardless of religious beliefs or affiliation. What makes this organization unique is that they offer their services free of charge. It is not necessary to join or pay any membership dues to secure their services should you ever find it necessary to use them. The organization exists solely on donations.

The Rutherford Institute has a proven track record in their defense of homeschool families. They have a separate department that deals with education matters and a staff of knowledgeable attorneys who keep current on home education issues.

TRI realizes that in protecting our rights they are also protecting their rights and protecting America from being stolen away from us. Whether or not you ever need the services of this organization, I recommend you consider donating to help them fight the battles that will secure our First Amendment rights. You can hear John Whitehead on Christian radio stations around America as he announces current First Amendment concerns on his brief, daily report called Freedom Under Fire. To contact, donate, or to request their newsletter, ACTION, use the information below.

The Rutherford Institute
P.O. Box 7482, Charlottesville, VA 22906
Phone: (804) 978-3888 / Fax: (804) 978-1789
e-mail: rutherford@fni.com
www.rutherford.org

THE HOMESCHOOL LEGAL DEFENSE ASSOCIATION (HSLDA)

In 1983, attorney Michael Farris founded the HSLDA. This Christian-based organization was instrumental in helping many states secure their homeschool laws. It's main purpose is to provide legal counsel and, if necessary, representation to homeschool families in a cost-effective manner. It accomplishes this by bringing together large numbers of homeschool families who pay a membership to a common fund. The membership fee is $100 per year per family with discounts for groups of 25 families or more, joining at the same time. It is important that you apply for and attain membership before a crisis occurs since their policy allows them to represent current members only. Christianity is not required for membership.

Member services include, among other things, full payment of all attorney's fees by the Association. Many times, however, intervention (such as a letter or call from one of their attorneys) will be enough to rectify the situation and avoid litigation. Your membership dues also entitle you to receive their quarterly newsletter with in-depth legal updates.

You can call or write HSLDA for an information brochure and application form which includes more details.

HSLDA
P.O. Box 159, Paeonian Springs, VA 20129
Phone: (540) 338-5600 / Fax: (540) 338-2733
e-mail: mailroom@hslda.org / website: www.hslda.org

HSLDA of Canada
2-3295 Dunmore Road, SE, Medicine Hat, AB T1B3R2
Phone: (403) 986-3400 / Fax: (403) 529-2694
e-mail: hslda@mlc.awinc.com

National Center for Home Education
P.O. Box 125, Paeonian Springs, VA 22129
Phone: (540) 338-5600 Fax: (540) 338-9333
A national support organization for state support groups.
This organization monitors legislative developments and
notifies state leaders. It also hosts an annual leadership
conference. This is a division of HSLDA and
directed by attorney, Chris Klicka.

National Home Education Research Institute
(NHERI)
P.O. Box 13939, Salem, OR 97309
(503) 364-1490
e-mail: mail@nheri.org.
Provides the most current and accurate research findings
concerning homeschooling.

LOCAL SUPPORT GROUPS — THEIR FUNCTION AND PURPOSE

It would be impossible for me to even attempt to list all the local support groups across the country. But with a little detective work you can be on the phone with a fellow homeschooler in your town in a matter of minutes. Call your state organization and ask for a support group contact person from your area. If there isn't a support group close by or they don't have a listing, they may be willing to give you an individual member's name and phone number. Don't be surprised if they don't give out individual names, however, because many have policies against it to protect their members. If they won't give you a name then give them your name and number and ask them to contact the member for you. All you have to do is wait for a return phone call. Veteran home-schoolers are notorious encouragers and helpers to new home-schoolers. They remember, all too well, when they were in your shoes and they are happy to be on the giving end.

Once you've checked out the support groups in your area you will find that every support group has its own personality. Some have grown quite large and are open for anyone who would like to join, while others prefer to limit their size to maintain intimacy among the members. Some are strictly Christian, while some are secular, and still others operate under Judeo-Christian beliefs but have their general membership open to anyone. Some operate strictly with volunteer workers, while others have a paid staff. Each of these support groups serve a vital role in encouraging and supporting homeschool parents.

I would encourage you to join a local support group and your state organization. If there are no support groups in your area, why not consider starting one? It only takes two families to begin. Soon your support group, with its own personality, will be a blessing to you and the other families involved.

FUNCTIONS OF A TYPICAL SUPPORT GROUP

As mentioned earlier, no two support groups are the same nor do they all offer the same services. When joining a support group, or if you begin your own, remember that rarely will all of the following functions be present in any one group. The volunteer leaders or staff must decide how much time they are willing to commit and then build their services from that perspective. Be prepared to pay some membership dues. Most support groups, even volunteer groups, charge a fee to cover operating costs, i.e. printing, postage, office supplies, etc.

FUNCTIONS:

1. To provide support and encouragement to its members.
2. To disseminate proper information regarding the law, how to begin homeschooling, and how to maintain an effective home-school.
3. To furnish ongoing information and instruction by providing newsletters and monthly, bi-monthly, or even weekly support group meetings featuring guest speakers or knowledgeable parents from within the organization.
4. To sponsor annual or occasional seminars featuring well-known homeschooling authorities.

5. To sponsor local field trips for the children on a weekly or monthly basis.

6. To provide extracurricular activities and events such as spelling bees, science fairs, language arts festivals, talent nights, art/music/dance classes, Presidential Physical Fitness tryouts, promotion and awards ceremonies, Junior/Senior Banquets, children's literary newspapers, etc.

7. To provide or sponsor testing and evaluations.

8. To hold annual curriculum fairs for curriculum distributors to display what they have available to homeschoolers.

9. To act as a liaison between the homeschool group and the school board.

I cannot overemphasize the importance of a support group in your homeschooling experience. Your effectiveness as a home educator may some day hinge on having the encouragement of other like-minded people. Remember, as a member your role is not only to glean from all the wonderful activities, but also to do your part to support others within your organization. Sometimes veteran homeschoolers forget how much the support group helped them when they were novices, and stop attending meetings and functions because they feel they are at a point where they do not require as much support. It is at that very time that the new homeschoolers need that person's wealth of wisdom and they are no where to be found. Find out from your leader what you can do to be an effective support group member.

APPENDIX B

RESOURCE AND CURRICULUM SUPPLIERS

The following is a list of suppliers listed in alphabetical order by publishers' names or suppliers' names. This is by no means an exhaustive list. If you need a more complete listing refer to Cathy Duffy's books, *The Christian Home Educator's Curriculum Manual: Elementary Grades* or *Junior/Senior High Grades* ($19.95 each) and/or Mary Pride's *Big Book of Home Learning: Volume 1 - Getting Started, Volume 2 - Preschool/Elementary,* and *Volume 3 - Teen and College* ($25.00 each volume). Both are available from general home school mail-order catalog companies.

GENERAL HOME SCHOOL MAIL-ORDER CATALOG COMPANIES

These companies carry a wide variety of curriculum. Their product choices typically reflect their philosophy of home education. Their teaching tips and reviews make acquiring each one of these catalogs beneficial. Share the cost with a friend (or friends) by requesting the catalogs on postcards bearing all of your names and addresses. Here is a list of the companies. See below for the contact information.

Lifetime Books and Gifts	Elijah Company
Noble Publishing	Greenleaf Press
Shekinah Curriculum Cellar	Family Christian Academy
Sycamore Tree	Timberdoodle Company
Builder Books	God's World Publications
Rainbow Resource Center	Hearthside Home School Helps

In defense of the small businesses: Please remember if you benefit from the advice and help of a retail company you should also make your purchases with them. When you purchase from a discounter who hasn't serviced you, you are contributing to the demise of the small businesses who specialize in personal service. Most of these companies are homeschoolers with advice and wisdom you don't want to lose. And, if you don't want to receive the "Uncouth Award," remember to never, ever walk into a company's booth at a convention, "pick their brain" (ask for service), and then compare their prices with a discounter's catalog in hand. That is considered *very* uncool. These vendors must pay for booth space to be present to serve you. Please re-pay them by patronizing their businesses.

KEY TO SYMBOLS

After some of the publishers' names you will see one to five symbols listed. If a symbol does not appear at all, it means that particular curriculum does not fall under any of the following categories. Please read the following to understand this symbol system.

C = Correspondence School or Prepared Curriculum

If you don't like the idea of picking, choosing, and putting together your own curriculum, then these companies will send you a package of all of the books for a grade level. Be careful, though, because many children work on different grade levels in the various subjects. If you suspect your child fits that category, check for a company which will customize the curriculum to your child's needs. Some of these companies require all the work to be sent back to them for grading and documentation. Some provide phone counseling.

SS= School Services

While similar to correspondence schools, these organizations usually allow you more freedom to pick and choose your home-school materials based on your philosophy of education. The services they perform are varied but generally they provide phone assistance (especially for beginners), maintain records, provide testing, evaluate your child's work, and sometimes provide transcripts or diplomas.

P = Paced Programs

"Paces" are instructional materials in worktext form. This means the informational text material is included in the workbook. The child can "pace" himself and complete as many worktexts as he feels motivated to do. The child reads the material, answers the questions, takes a test, and moves on to the next pace. Most of these are self-instructional and require limited parental involvement. It requires much rote memorization and our experience shows that children become bored with it rather quickly.

* = Sells Books Separately

These companies will sell books, supplies, etc. separately even if you are not enrolled in their correspondence course and/ or are not buying their prepared programs. This symbol will only be used in conjunction with the symbol "C" and "S" when applicable.

H = High School Programs

These are accredited high school programs that issue a diploma upon successfully completing their program. This diploma is accepted in all colleges and armed forces.

A Beka Book Publications (C*)
P.O. Box 19100, Pensacola, FL 32523-9100
(800) 874-2352
— Christian, K - 12

Abrams, Harry N., Inc.
100 Fifth Ave., New York, NY 10011
(800) 288-2131

Addison-Wesley Publishing Company
1 Jacob Way, Reading MA 01867
(800) 358-4566 / FAX (800) 367-7198

Alpha Omega Publications (P*)
300 N. McKinney Ave., Chandler, AZ 85226
(800) 622-3070
— Christian, K -12

American Christian History Institute
James Rose
P.O. Box 648, Palo Cedro, CA 96073
(530) 547-3535

American School (C,H)
2200 East 170 Street, Lansing, IL 60438
(708) 418-2800
— Secular

Aristoplay (Games for Fun and Learning)
P.O. 7028, Ann Arbor, MI 48107
(734) 995-4353

Audio Memory Publishing
501 Cliff Drive, Newport Beach, CA 92663
(800) 365-SING

Backyard Scientist
P.O. Box 16966, Irvine, CA 92713

Bob Jones University Press (C *)
Greenville, SC 29614
(800) 845-5731
— Christian, K - 12

Builder Books
P.O. Box 99, Riverside, WA 98849
(800) 260-5461 (orders only)
(509) 826-6021

Calvert School (C)
105 Tuscany Road, Baltimore, MD 21210
(410) 243-6030 / FAX (410) 366-0674
— Secular, K - 12

Cambridge Academy (C)
3855 SE Lake Weir, Ocala, FL 34480
(800) 252-3777

Castlemoyle Books
6701 180th Street SW, Lynnwood, WA 98037
(425) 787-2714 / FAX (425) 787-0631

Charlotte Mason Research
and Supply Company
P.O. Box 936, Elkton, MD 21922-0936

Christian Liberty Academy (C*)
502 W. Euclid Ave., Arlington Hts, IL 60004
(800) 348-0899
— Christian, K - 12

Christian Light Education (C*,P)
P.O. Box 1212, Harrisonburg, VA 22801
(540) 434-0750
— Mennonite, K - 12

Clonlara School Home Based
Education Program (SS)
1289 Jewett Avenue, Ann Arbor, MI 48104
(734) 769-4515

Common Sense Press
P.O. Box 1365, 8786 Hwy 21, Melrose, FL 32666
(352) 475-5757

Concerned Communications
P.O. Box 1000, Siloam Springs, AR 72761
(501) 549-9000

Cornerstone Curriculum Project
2006 Flat Creek, Richardson, TX 75080
(972) 235-5149

Design-a-Study
408 Victoria Avenue, Wilmington, DE 19804
(302) 998-3889

D.P. & K. Productions
1285 Morgan Springs Rd., Dayton, TN 37321
(423) 570-7172

EDC Publishing (Usborne Books)
P.O. Box 470663 Tulsa, OK 74147
(800) 475-4522

Education PLUS+
P.O. Box 1350, Taylors, SC 29687
(864) 609-5411

Education Services
8825 Blue Mountain Dr., Golden, CO 80403
(303) 234-5245
(Ruth Beechick materials)

Elijah Company, The
1053 Eldridge Loop
Crossville, TN 38558
(931) 456-6284 / FAX (931) 456-6384

EPS - Educators Publishing Service
31 Smith Place, Cambridge, MA 02138
(800) 225-5750 / (617) 547-6706 in MA

Eternal Hearts
P.O. Box 107, Colville, WA 99114
(509) 732-4147

Family Christian Academy
487 Myatt Dr., Madison, TN 37115
(615) 860-3000 / FAX (615) 860-9475

Ferg N Us Services
PO Box 350, Richville, NY 13681
(315) 287-9131 / FAX (315) 287-9132

Foundation for American
Christian Education (F.A.C.E.)
Info on the Principle Approach
P.O. Box 9588, Chesapeake, VA 23321
(757) 488-6601

Frank Schaffer
P.O. Box 2853, Torrance, CA 90509-2853
ORDERS (800) 421-5565 / FAX (800) 837-7260

God's World Publications
P.O. Box 2330, Asheville, NC 28802-2330
(800) 951-5437 / FAX (828) 253-1556

Greenleaf Press
3761 Hwy 109 N - Unit D, Lebanon, TN 37087
(615) 449-1617

Harthun, Kim R. (Science Fair Manual)
6328 East Sweetwater Dr., Lakeland, FL 33813
(941) 619-7954

Hearthside Home School Helps
74 Lynn Drive, Woodbury, NJ 08096
(609) 845-3681 / EMAIL hearthside@juno.com

Hewitt Home Schooling Resources (SS)
P.O. Box 9, Washougal, WA 98671
(800) 348-1750

Home Computer Market, The
P.O. Box 385377, Bloomington, MN 55438
(800) 450-7298 ext. 0516

Home Life (Mary Pride)
P.O. Box 1250, Fenton, MO 63026
(800) 346-6322

Home Run Enterprises /
Grove Publishing (Cathy Duffy)
16172 Huxley Circle, Westminster, CA 92683
(714) 841-1220

Homeschooling Seminars and Publications
182 N. Columbus Heights Road
Longview, WA 98632
(360) 423-4912

Home Study International (C)
P.O. Box 4437, Silver Spring, MD 20914-4437
(800) 782-4769

How Great Thou ART
P.O. Box 48, McFarland, NC 28102
(800) 982-3729

International Learning Systems
at North America
1000-112 Circle North, Suite 100
St. Petersburg, FL 33716
(800) 321-8322

John Holt's Book and Music Store Catalog
2380 Massachusetts Avenue, Suite 104
Cambridge, MA 02140
(617) 864-3100

Key Curriculum Press
1150- 65th Street, Emeryville, CA 94608
(800) 338-7638

KONOS Character Curriculum
P.O. Box 250, Anna, TX 75409
(972) 924-2712 / FAX (972) 924-2701

Learning Potentials Publishers
230 W. Main St., Lewisville, TX 75057
(800) 437-7976

Learning Power
P.O. Box 770253, Coral Springs, FL 33077
Phone: (954) 726-2671 / FAX (954) 724-9884

Lifetime Books and Gifts
Bob and Tina Farewell
3900 Chalet Suzanne Lane
Lake Wales, FL 33853
(941) 676-6311 / FAX (941) 676-2732

McGraw-Hill
220 East Danieldale Road, DeSoto, TX 75115
(800) 843-8855

McGregor, Debora
2954 Shell Rd., Lake Wales, FL 33853
(941) 678-3454

Modern Curriculum Press
P.O. Box 2649, Columbus, OH 43216
(800) 321-3106

Moore Foundation and
Moore Academy (SS)
P.O. Box 1, Camas, WA 98607
(360) 835-2736

Mott Media
1000 East Huron, Milford, MI 48381
(248) 685-8773

National Home Education Research Inst.
P.O. Box 13939, Salem, OR 97309
(503) 364-1490 / e-mail: mail@nheri.org.

National Writing Institute
7946 Wright Road, Niles, MI 49120
(800) 688-5375 / FAX (616) 684-5375

Noble Publishing
P.O. Box 2250, Gresham, OR 97030
(503) 667-3942

North Dakota State University —
Division of Independent Studies (C*H)
P.O.Box 5036, Fargo, ND 58105
(701) 231-6000
— Secular

Oral Roberts University College Program /
Home Education Center
7777 S. Lewis Ave., Tulsa, OK 74171
(918) 495-6621

Prentice Hall / Simon & Schuster
P.O. Box 11071, Des Moines, IA 50336
(800) 947-7700

Rainbow Resource Center
Rt. 1 Box 159A-50N 500 E Rd., Toulon, IL 61483
(309) 695-3105 / FAX (309) 695-3042

Rod and Staff Publishers (C *)
P.O. Box 3, Highway 172, Crockett, KY 41413
(606) 522-4348
— Mennonite, K - 12

Saxon Publishers, Inc. (C *)
2450 John Saxon Blvd., Norman, OK 73071
(800) 284-7019, ext. 1651
— Secular, math texts, K - 12

School of Tomorrow (P)
P.O. Box 299000, Lewisville, TX 75029-9000
(800) 925-7777
— Christian, K/3 - 12

Seton Home Study Catholic Curriculum (C)
1350 Progress Drive, Front Royal, VA 22630
(540) 636-9990

Shekinah Curriculum Cellar
101 Meador Road, Kilgore, TX 75662
(903) 643-2760 / FAX (903) 643-2796

Singing Springs Productions
Monte and Karey Swan
7072 Singing Springs Lane, Evergreen, CO 80439
Phone:(303) 670-0673 / FAX: (303) 674-3431

Summit Christian Academy (C*)
2100 North Highway 360, Suite 503
Grand Prairie, TX 75050
(800) 362-9180

The Sycamore Tree School (SS*)
2179 Meyer Place, Costa Mesa, CA 92627
(949) 650-4466 / ORDERS (800) 779-6750
$3 catalog with great home education supplies.

Timberdoodle
1510 E. Spencer Lake Rd., Shelton, WA 98584
(360) 426-0672 / FAX ORDERS (800) 478-0672

World Book, Inc.
100 E. Campus View Blvd., Suite 370
Columbus, OK 43235
(800) 621-8202

University of Nebraska (C * H)
Depart. of Distance Education - NCEE
33 & Holdridge Streets, Room 269
Lincoln, Nebraska 68583-9800
(402) 472-4321 / FAX (402) 472-1901
— Secular

Weekly Reader Corporation
3001 Cindel Drive, Delran, NJ 08370
(800) 446-3355

APPENDIX C

———•◆•———

HELPFUL BOOKS AND RESOURCES FOR PARENTS

Many of these excellent books have been listed throughout this manual. They have been compiled here for your convenience. Unless otherwise indicated, they are available through general homeschool mail-order catalogs. See Appendix B.

Anyone Can Homeschool, by Terry Dorian and Zan Peters Tyler
Cost: $10.99
> The authors inspire our confidence to successfully homeschool and then explain how to find what works for us through an examination of the philosophies of education.

Art of the Homeschool Lifestyle, The, by Karey Swan
> This promises to be a pivotal book on the issue of The Learning Lifestyle. Karey is a kindred spirit on this concept and we've spent many hours "philosophizing" about it. It is still being written so keep your eye out for it.

Beyond Survival, by Diana Waring
Cost: $12.99
> Gives you the preparation and working plan for a successful homeschooling experience. Diana takes you on her family's delightful homeschool journey and includes plenty of humor along the way.

Big Book of Home Learning, The, by Mary Pride
Cost: $25.00 each
> *Volume 1: Getting Started, Volume 2: Preschool/Elementary*, and *Volume 3: Teen and College.*

A directory with review of just about every curriculum available to the homeschooler.

Books Children Love, by Elizabeth Wilson
Cost: $13.99
A guide to children's literature based on Charlotte Mason's definition of "living books."

Christian Home Educator's Curriculum Manual, by Cathy Duffy
(Elementary or Jr./Sr. High)
General availability or Home Run Enterprises
Cost: $19.95 each volume
A thorough listing with reviews of practically every curriculum available to homeschoolers. Full of teaching tips and complete information on learning styles.

Christian Home School, The, by Gregg Harris
Cost: $12.95
A book for Christian families that teaches how to homeschool on a solidly biblical foundation.

Dumbing Us Down, by John Taylor Gatto
Cost: $9.95
Written by the New York State Teacher of the Year. A startling account of how and why the methods of compulsory state education are failing America's children.

For the Children's Sake, by Susan Schaeffer Macaulay
Cost: $8.99
A consolidation of the writings of Charlotte Mason and describes what education was meant to be. Inspirational!

Going Home to School, by Llewellyn Davis
Cost: $12.99
Answers to why we homeschool. Exposes the humanistic philosophy of the public schools and the problems with the private Christian schools. Written from a Christian perspective.

Hearth and Home, by Karey Swan
Cost: $17.00

Find the time to enjoy homemaking life skills that go beyond maintenance. This is a recipe book that goes beyond recipes into the philosophy of the homeschool lifestyle.

Hidden Art of Homemaking: Creative Ideas for Enriching Everyday Life, by Edith Schaeffer
Cost: $9.99

How to make our home the center of meaningful living and personal enrichment through the simple creative touch.

Home Education: Rights and Reasons, by John Whitehead
Cost: $16.95

Written by the founder of The Rutherford Institute it explains your legal rights and the reasons many of us homeschool. Also contains legislative summaries of all fifty states.

Home Grown Kids, by Dr. and Mrs. Raymond Moore
Cost: $9.00

Practical how-to's of homeschooling with statistics to back up your reasons for wanting to homeschool.

Home Schooling For Excellence, by David and Micki Colfax
Cost: $10.99

The delightful, real-life story of a family who allowed their children to pursue their interests in learning which resulted in Harvard and Yale scholarships.

Home School Manual, The, by Ted Wade
Cost: $19.95

Covers the gamut in home education.

Home Style Teaching, by Dr. Raymond and Dorothy Moore
Cost: $10.00

This book, along with *Home Grown Kids*, was the "how-to homeschool" book back in the early 80's. Most veterans cut their homeschool teeth on this book and probably still refer to it, like I do.

Homeschooling Father, The Key to Success and Sanity, The,
by Michael Farris
Cost: $ 6.95
> Discusses why the father is the key to successful homeschooling. Recommended by my husband, Jack.

Honey for a Child's Heart, by Gladys Hunt
Cost: $10.99
> A Christian guide to children's literature

How to Home School: A Practical Approach, by Gayle Graham
Cost: $20.00
> The "how-tos" of teaching unit studies and the 3 R's. Excellent resource for those teaching via unit studies.

How to Tutor, by Samuel Blumenfeld
Cost: $19.95
> Teaches you how to teach the 3 R's.

Hurried Child, The, by David Elkind
Check your library or local bookstore.
> A proponent of delayed academics. Exposes the consequences to our children when they are forced to perform academically or socially before they are ready to handle the pressures.

KONOS: Creating the Balance, Video Series with Jessica Hulcy
Available through KONOS, Inc.
Cost: $150.00
> A comprehensive "how-to homeschool" seminar which not only teaches how to use the KONOS Curriculum, but gives practical advice for balancing homeschool responsibilities with the rest of life. Contact your KONOS representative for a group showing at a lower cost.

Language Wars and Other Writings for Homeschoolers, The,
by Ruth Beechick
Cost: $16.00

continued on following page

Another source to help you think through the myriad of available curricula by an educator who encourages us to trust in our children's God-given ability to learn.

Learning All the Time, by John Holt
Cost: $11.00
John Holt's beliefs about how children learn and how parents can help them.

Margin, by Dr. Richard Swenson, M.D.
Cost: $12.00
Reveals how we can restore emotional, physical, financial, and time reserves to our overloaded lives. See the Epilogue for more regarding *Margin*.

Read Aloud Handbook, The, by Jim Trelease
Cost: $11.00
Compelling reasons for reading aloud forever and a proven "Treasury of Books" to choose from.

Read for Your Life, by Gladys Hunt and Barbara Hampton
Cost: $9.99
A Christian guide to literature for the teenager.

Relaxed Home School, The, by Mary Hood
Cost: $10.95
Shows us how to allow our children to learn by pursuing their interests.

Right Choice - Home Schooling, The, by Chris Klicka
Cost: $13.95
Exposes the failure and dangers of the public school system and reveals how homeschooling is the answer for our children and our nation.

Successful Home School Family Handbook, The,
by Dr. and Mrs. Raymond Moore
Cost: $13.00

To help you implement a creative and stress free approach to homeschooling. Many testimonials by moms who have successfully used their formula.

Teach Your Own, by John Holt
Check libraries or John Holt's Book and Music Store Catalog
 The original reference on the "Unschooling Approach."

Teaching Children, by Diane Lopez
Cost: $12.99
 A scope and sequence (curriculum guide) for children through the 6th grade. Based on Charlotte Mason's educational philosophy.

Ten Mistakes Parents Make With Teenagers (And How To Avoid Them), By Jay Kesler
Christian Bookstore
Currently out of print
 Reading this book at the beginning of Tim's teenage years saved us from making the most common parental mistakes (well — many of them). The teens have been the best years yet!

Three R's Series, The, by Dr. Ruth Beechick
Cost: $12.00/ pack of 3 or $4.00 each
 Includes *A Home Start in Reading, An Easy Start In Arithmetic, A Strong Start in Language* (all for grades K - 3).

What is a Family?, by Edith Schaeffer
Cost: $12.99
 A touching reminder of what the family should be.

What Kids Need Most in a Dad, by Tim Hansel
Cost: $8.95
 Not specifically homeschool-related but very dad-related. Assists you dads in the task of being the kind of father your children depend on you to be. Christian perspective. This is Jack's recommendation!

WholeHearted Child, The, by Clay and Sally Clarkson
Cost: $20.95

> The Clarkson's present "Home-Centered Learning" as their favored method to raising a whole-hearted Christian child. Whole books and life experience are emphasized.

You CAN Teach Your Child Successfully, by Dr. Ruth Beechick
Cost: $14.00

> A detailed, "how-to" scope and sequence for grades 4 - 8. Must reading!

PARENT'S MAGAZINES AND NEWSLETTERS REGARDING HOMESCHOOLING

Most of these will provide you with a sample issue for $3.00.

Acts and Facts
Institute for Creation Research
P.O. Box 2667, El Cajon, CA 92021-0667
Cost: Free, but donations appreciated.

> Updates on current research regarding creationism.

Growing Without Schooling
2269 Massachusetts Ave., Cambridge, MA 02140
Cost: $25.00 annual subscription. Arrives monthly.
Group memberships available; request current information

> Newsletter reflecting John Holt's philosophy of unschooling. Secular perspective.

Home School Digest
Wisdom Publications, Box 575, Winona Lake, IN 46590
Cost: $18.00 annual subscription. Arrives quarterly.

> Deals with the deeper spiritual and philosophical issues of homeschooling.

Homeschooling Today
P.O. Box 5863, Hollywood, FL 33083 / (954) 962-1930
Cost: $17.95/annual subscription. Arrives bi-monthly.

Wonderfully unique magazine breaking from the traditional covering of the philosophy of home education and instead gives usable unit studies, activities, and curriculum ideas in the areas of art, science, math, language arts, teen programs, and more.

How to Home School Newsletter
5903 Grove Ave., Richmond, VA 23226
Cost: 4 postage stamps
> Features tips and advice from Gayle Graham, author of *How to Home School: A Practical Approach*

The Moore Report International
Box 1, Camas, WA 98607
Cost: $12.00/annual subscription. Arrives bi-monthly.
> Subtitled: *Authoritative Family Briefs for Busy People.* A brief newsletter to keep you updated on research, legislative news, seminars, and more.

NATHHAN News
5383 Alpine Rd. SE, Olalla, WA 98359
(206)857-4257 or FAX (206)857-7764
Cost: $25 donation published quarterly
> A Christian non-profit organization dedicated to providing encouragement to families with special-needs children who are homeschooling.

Parent's Review Magazine
The Charlotte Mason Research and Supply Company
P.O. Box 936, Elkton, MD 21922-0936
> Includes articles from Mason's original PR as well as articles from families using this method today.

Patriarch Magazine, edited by Phil Lancaster
P.O. Box 50, Willis, VA 24380
(540) 745-6433
Cost: By Donation. Suggested Donation:
        $25/yr - print, $30/yr - audio
        Sample: $4 - print, $5 - audio
    Articles for men on raising a family and homeschooling from a
    Biblical perspective.

Practical Homeschooling
Home Life, P.O. Box 1250, Fenton, MO 63026-1850
1-800-346-6322 (credit card orders only)
FAX (314) 343-7203, or email PHSCustSvc@AOL.com.
Cost: $19.95 for six issues (one year); $35 for 12 issues (2 years)
    Written from a Christian perspective and includes a wide variety
    of feature articles, special columnists, and curriculum reviews.

Quit You Like Men
152 Maple Lane, Harriman, TN 37748
Phone/FAX: (423) 346-7824 / e-mail: JiBarber@highland.net
Cost: $24.00/1-year; $45.00/2-year; $64.00/3-year (6 issues/year)
    Articles for men concerning homeschooling and homesteading.
    Particular emphasis on homesteading and home businesses.

Relaxed Home Schooler, The, edited by Mary Hood
P.O. Box 2524, Cartersville, GA 30120 / (770) 917-9141
Cost: FREE!
    Features tips and advice from the author of *The Relaxed Home
    School*.

Teaching Home Magazine, The
12311 NE Brazee, Portland, OR 97230
Cost: $15.00/annual subscription. Arrives bi-monthly.
    Written from a Christian perspective. Price includes a state
    newsletter inside the magazine.

Teaching the Trivium

Trivium Pursuit, 139 Colorado St. Suite 168, Muscatine, IA 52761
(309) 537-3641 or www.muscanet.com/~trivium
Cost: $9.00 quarterly. They suggest purchasing year one's issues
first ($9) since these were written sequentially.

The Classical Approach to Christian education; explained and applied to homeschooling

CHILDREN'S MAGAZINES
TO SUPPLEMENT CURRICULUM

Clubhouse, Clubhouse Jr., *Brio* and *Breakaway*

Focus on the Family,
P.O. Box 35500, Colorado Springs, CO 80935
Cost: $15.00 Annual subscription. Arrives monthly.

Articles emphasize scriptural principles. *Clubhouse Jr.* for ages 6 to 8. *Clubhouse* for ages 8 to 12. *Brio* for teen girls and *Breakaway* for teen guys.

Cobblestone: The History Magazine for Young People

P.O. Box 6991, Syracuse, NY 13217 / (800) BUGPALS
Cost: Approx. $20.00/annual subscription. Arrives monthly.

Each issue deals with one topic from American history. For ages 8 - 11.

Cricket: The Magazine for Children

P.O. Box 51144, Boulder, CO 80321
Cost: Approx. $22.50/annual subscription. Arrives monthly.

A literary magazine for children ages 6 - 12.

God's World

P.O. Box 2330, Asheville, NC 28802-2330 / (800) 951-5437
Cost: $18-$20 for 26 issues, delivered from September to May.

A weekly current events newspaper for ages K-12. Written from a Christian perspective. Group rates available upon request.

Kids Art

P.O. Box 274 Mt. Shasta, CA 96067 / (916) 926-5076
Cost: $10.00 for quarterly publications.

Full of art projects, history, and appreciation of art.

National Geographic World
Dept. 00187, 17th and M St. NW, Washington, DC 20036
Cost: $9.95/annual subscription. Arrives monthly.
General interest with nature-related articles for ages 8 -13.

Nature's Friend
P.O. Box 22777, SR 119, Goshen, Indiana 46526 / (219) 534-2245
Cost: $22.00/annual subscription. Arrives monthly.
Nature articles with Christian perspective for ages 4 - 13.

Odyssey
P.O. Box 92788, Milwaukee, WI 53202
Cost: $21.00/annual subscription. Arrives monthly.
A space exploration and astronomy magazine for ages 8 - 12.

Ranger Rick
National Wildlife Federation
8925 Leesburg Pike, Vienna VA 22184-0001 / (800) 432-6564
Cost: $14.00/annual subscription. Arrives monthly.
A nature magazine for ages 8 - 12.

Your Big Backyard
National Wildlife Federation, 1412-16th St. NW
Washington, DC 20036
Cost: $10.00/annual subscription. Arrives monthly.
A nature magazine primarily about animals. For preschoolers.

Weekly Reader
3001 Cindel Drive, Delran, NJ 08370 / (800) 446-3355
Cost: $24.95 for 28 issues per year
A current events newspaper for children in Pre-K - 6th grade.
Includes posters and map-a-month. Secular perspective.

ZooBooks
Wildlife Education Limited
9820 Willowcreek Road, Suite 300, San Diego, CA 92131
Cost: About $15/annual subscription. 10 issues.
A science/nature magazine with an emphasis on animals.

APPENDIX D

——•◆•——

HOW TO USE THE RECORD-KEEPING FORMS

Since this book is not a standard 8½ x 11 size, you may wish to copy the forms on a machine that can enlarge by 110%. This will provide you with the correct size to fit a standard binder.

Form A is used to document the titles of books your children have read such as library books, textbooks, workbooks, magazines, newspapers, encyclopedia selections, the Bible, and others. If your child is a non-reader, you would list the books you are reading to him. Keep in mind, you are free to "not list" anything you wish. If a list of books is required by your state you can combine this with any of the forms below to fulfill compliance.

Form B will require the use of one page for each day of instruction. This form allows you to separate each subject and describe in detail what took place each day. To save time, write in your subject titles before copying this form.

Form C covers one week at a time. This form allows you to briefly describe each subject individually. To save time, write in your subject titles before copying.

Form D is a two-page form and is used on a weekly basis. It provides a space for a brief description of your activities and a larger space to the right to document the reading materials in specific categories. In the "books" column titled Library and Other Books Read and Used for Subject Matter, you should list titles of textbooks, workbooks, Bible and so on. Before copying, write in the titles of books you use every week to save time. The two pages will face each other inside your notebook or a 3-ring binder. The bottom right corner is marked (L) or (R) meaning the page belongs on the left or right side.

Form E is simply the same as Form D except without subject titles or categories written in the spaces. You can use the area to the right to keep an expanded journal for the week or your child can write his journal in that area. To save time, write in subject titles before copying.

Form F will require the use of one page for each day of instruction allowing you to list your reading materials and your activities on the same form. This will be advantageous for those who integrate their subjects and do not care to separate the activities into subject categories.

Form G is the same as Form F except it is for weekly use. This is for those who wish to keep records on a weekly basis (like me) rather than a daily basis.

Form H is a weekly planner for those who choose to teach the Unit Study method and wish to keep all their plans on one page. These planners can double as your records. See Chapter Two for a complete discussion on Unit Studies.

Another Alternative is to simply keep a daily or weekly journal. Entries could be made by both parent and child. Again, make sure this will comply with your state's laws.

Student:

Date	Title of Reading Material Used	Author	Comments

Daily Log

Student: **Date:**

Subjects	Descriptions

Student: _____

Week of _____

Subjects	Monday	Tuesday	Wednesday	Thursday	Friday

Form C

Subject	Monday	Tuesday	Wednesda
English / Handwriting			
Spelling			
Math			
Social Studies			
Science			
Arts & Music			
Physical Development			
Spiritual Development			

Form D(L)

Thursday	Friday	Student:
		Week of
		Library & Other Books Read & Used for Subject Matter
		1)
		2)
		3)
		4)
		5)
		6)
		7)
		8)
		9)
		10)
		11)
		12)
		13)
		14)
		15)
		Books Read for Leisure by Child
		1)
		2)
		3)
		4)
		5)
		6)
		7)
		8)
		9)
		10)
		Books Read for Leisure to Child (by Adult)
		1)
		2)
		3)
		4)
		5)
		6)
		7)
		8)
		9)
		10)

Form D(R)

Subject	Monday	Tuesday	Wednesda

Form E(L)

Thursday	Friday

Student:

Week of

Journal by:

Daily Log

Student: _____ **Date:** _____

Titles of Reading Material Used	Author	Titles of Reading Material Used	Author
1)		6)	
2)		7)	
3)		8)	
4)		9)	
5)		10)	

Activities Performed Today Were:

Student: ⠀⠀⠀⠀⠀⠀⠀⠀⠀⠀⠀⠀⠀⠀⠀⠀⠀⠀⠀ **Date:**

Titles of Reading Material Used	Author	Titles of Reading Material Used	Author
1)		9)	
2)		10)	
3)		11)	
4)		12)	
5)		13)	
6)		14)	
7)		15)	
8)		16)	

Activities Performed This Week Were:

Unit Study Planner

Unit Topic:

Week of _____

Bible References:

Vocabulary Words:

Book Titles:

Writing Projects:

Activities:

Day 5 (Hands-On Day)

Field Trips:

Supplies Needed:

Day 1

Day 2

Day 3

Day 4

INDEX

NOTES

NOTES